The Reluctant Dog Trainer

philip McCarlie-Davis

Published by philip McCarlie-Davis, 2021.

THE RELUCTANT DOG TRAINER

First edition. August 6, 2021.

Copyright © 2021 philip McCarlie-Davis.

ISBN: 979-8201535148

Written by philip McCarlie-Davis.

Contents

Introduction

A reluctant dog trainer

I did not set out to have a career working with dogs, nor did I aspire to working with animals of any sort. I left school fully intending to enjoy a life as a beach bum, painting and being "creative", however, living on the west coast of Wales I quickly discovered that to be a successful beach bum required a large budget for waterproofs and fleecy jackets. it was clear that I was going to have find something else to do with my life. It was at that point I attempted to join the rest of the world and learn things, to become a productive member of society, and so I went dutifully to art college, only to find that this was not going to be the path to enlightenment I was seeking. Six months of painting random still lives and the odd bit of finger painting and it was clear another path would be required. During my time at college my real interest forced itself out, for every brief we were given I would find a way to squeeze an animal into it, whether it was a dog, a chimp or a bird, every painting reflected the subject that really interested me. At one point my tutor critiqued a piece that I had been working on, only to say, "now there aren't any tigers in Aberystwyth are there?" therefore my lack of real-life study negated the picture. I was not in college much longer after that. Back home I started volunteering for a small animal collection, then I was lucky enough to be offered a job as a trainer for an assistance dog charity. Since that day I have had the chance to work with all sorts of dogs all of whom leave a mark, some even physically, but all of them have a place in my understanding of behaviour and training.

For me training and behaviour are intricately linked, in that to train effectively you need to be well versed in the behaviour that you are being offered by the animal, whether that is a dog, a cat, a bird or whatever you are trying to train. Also, my experiences in education taught me that learning can be stressful, especially when you are being told that you were not right, people learn and understand things in different ways, therefore to me it was logical that animals do the same. to effectively train, I have always found that it is important to establish an understanding of what is motivating the behaviour in the first place. once you have established this fact you often find that telling the dog it got it wrong is ineffective, meaning that the best way to train is to let the dog know when it is getting it right.

A few years ago, I tried to hang up my training hat, and tried a life without a clicker in my hand, poo bags in my back pocket, or treats everywhere, however training would not leave me alone. I find myself back in art college, trying to expand my life in one direction whilst off to the side, a dog sits staring at me, with a clicker at its feet.

Turns out, after twenty years, I do not like the beach either.

About this book

There are many books, videos, podcasts, articles, and courses all concerned with the subject of dog training, it would seem therefore, that there is no need for yet another one. This is probably true, and I would always recommend that as an owner, starting out training your dog, then reading as much as possible and watching as many videos as you can on the subject of training is very worthwhile.

This book is intended to act as an introduction to the world of dog training. I have kept the scope of this book quite small, covering just the aspects as they relate to training. The reason for this is so that we can keep things nice and simple. For suggestions on resources that cover behaviour and welfare of dogs, then I have put a list of some recommendations at the end of the book.

Equally this is not intended to be a vast work on learning theory, it is simply a little book which aims to give its reader the inspiration, confidence, and skills to start training their dog at home.

Even though the focus of the book is primarily dogs, the skills involved can be used with almost any species, allowing the owner or carer to improve all aspects of the animal's life by training various behaviours which help reduce the animals stress, fear, and worry.

Owning and training a dog can be a very fulfilling and rewarding occupation, it is hoped that this book will go some way to helping you find inspiration and joy to train your dog with fun and encouragement.

The whole dog

Training forms part of the process of raising a happy, healthy dog. It is a particularly important element, however, there are many dogs which have never attended training classes, and when questioning the owner, they tell you that they have not consciously trained the dog beyond sit, down and stay. Yet these dogs walk nicely, greet people nicely, enjoy the

4

company of people and other dogs, and by all accounts make raising a dog appear to be the easiest thing in the world. This suggests that there are other elements at play, more than just the process of training. It would be reasonable to suggest that these are also the diet the dog is fed upon, the amount of exercise it receives, and the overall health of the dog, all these aspects play an important role in the creation of the dog we all aim to live with. However, there are other aspects which equally feed into this dynamic and in many ways, they are much more significant than whether or not your dog will come when you call it.

In my opinion, the one element which stands out above all the others is the dog's relationship with the owner and with the family that it lives with. This not only includes the daily interactions that take place, but also the environment in which the dog lives. Unfortunately there is not a simple one size fits all solution as to what makes the perfect environment for a dog, and is largely dictated by the needs of the individual, however there are some elements that as owners we have control over, these are things as simple as the amount of noise and activity that takes place in the home, how much rest the dog receives, the interactions of other members of the household, and whether the dog actually feels safe and secure in the environment in which it lives. All of these elements contribute to the dog's general sense of safety and security which form the foundations to the behaviours that we wish to see. For example, a dog which lives in a busy, distracting environment, may find it more difficult to focus its attention when trying to train even the most basic of behaviours. Failure to comply with the wishes of the owner, can lead to frustration building in both the trainer and the dog, subsequently leading to the dog learning sets of behaviours which the owner did not intend to train at all.

It is worth mentioning here that learning takes place all of the time, dogs are constantly taking in information, processing it, and learning from it, it is not the case that learning only occurs when there is food about, or when the owner attends a training class. From the minute the dog wakes up to the moment it goes to sleep it is learning how to deal with the world, how to secure the things that it requires to survive and so on. There is even a large amount of learning which takes place through the process of sleep, therefore with every interaction, the dog will take something away to use again at a later date when presented with the same cues and stimuli.

"Constructive coping strategies involve behavioural efforts designed to render an unfamiliar or threatening environment more predictable and controllable" (Lindsay, 2005)

.

It would not be possible to control every single element of the dog's day, and equally we would not want to, however, we can be aware of every interaction that we have and make decisions as to what the dog might learn from that interaction. For example, did the dog learn that you are a nice person first thing in the morning, or has it learned to avoid you first thing as it knows you are terribly grumpy until you have had your first cup of coffee. In an ideal world every interaction that we have with our dogs would be positive in nature and geared to teaching the dog something useful, however, unfortunately life has a habit of affecting how we ourselves interact with the world around us, and it would be almost impossible to be continually positive, therefore there will be the odd occasion where our reaction to the dog's behaviour, is less than we desired it to be. This is not the end of the world. If we have created a safe, secure, predictable environment, where the majority of interactions with the dog are positive, then the dog's ability to move through a negative experience will be that much greater. The dog's ability to rebound from adverse events is important, as there will be situations in the dog's life which occur that they do not enjoy very much. Where a dog has a stable relationship with their owner, their ability to bounce back is quicker and more solid. Where the relationship is not so stable, and the environment somewhat unpredictable, the dog's ability to recover can take much longer and the chances of them learning a set of behaviours in association to the event is much greater.

"Under the influence of positive efficacy expectancies, the dog is more likely to approach uncertain situations in a more confident, success-oriented, and adaptive way." (Lindsay, 2005)

Ideally, we would want our dogs to look to us for reassurance and guidance when they experience negative events (an unpleasant trip to the vet for example).

When we consider the whole dog, we need to look at the following elements.

- Training
- Environment
- Relationship
- Diet
- Health

Training

As mentioned above, dogs are learning constantly, it is our job as their owners to make sure that what they learn is conducive to helping them negotiate modern life, whether that is how to deal with new things, people, dogs, environments etc., or how to respond at the vets or the groomers and so on. Equally, we are required to explain the rules of the home to the dog from the earliest point. We should not expect our dogs to behave in the home if we have not explained to them the rules of the house. This is where training comes in.

There are a number of behaviours which are routinely trained, the foundation behaviours. Generally, these are considered to be Sit, down, Wait, stay, heel and recall. If our dogs learn these behaviours reliably, then they will be easier to control in the majority of situations that they will encounter. Often, once these behaviours have been established an owner will stop training formally (meaning, actually consciously engaging in the training process). Even though the dog will still be learning behaviours, whether the owner is aware of this or not.

When deciding what behaviours to train, I would always encourage an owner to list the behaviours that they find desirable, then ask themselves how those behaviours benefit the dog. With the foundation behaviours the benefit to the dog could be argued that with more control, the dog is safer in the environment, it is able to approach situations slower and reactivity is reduced. I would not argue with any of that; however, it may be possible to ask ourselves do we need the specific action to achieve the same end goal? For example, the action of sitting. For some dogs this may be an uncomfortable endeavor, maybe they are suffering hip pain, perhaps they are sore from running about a lot, with certain breeds the action itself may be uncomfortable, breeds such as greyhounds with their long spindly legs and long spines, may well prefer to stand instead of sitting.

That is not to say that these breeds will never sit, more that when we ask for behaviours such as sitting, we are not always conscious of how that behaviour is affecting the dog at that specific moment. Instead, we may simply teach a stand behaviour, or a wait behaviour. This would achieve the same end goal of arresting the dog's movement forward, and maintain them in a single space, but allows them the option to remain in a more comfortable position, especially if the required action is only needed momentarily, such as waiting at the side of the road.

Training itself is a great method of helping to bond with our dogs, it helps to build relationships, introduces predictability, and also allows us to explain the rules of life to our dogs. Training, when performed well, is one of the most effective methods of communicating with our dogs. There are other benefits also, if we forget about the fact that a trained dog is easier for us to handle, it is also the case that the process of training has significant benefits to the dogs welfare, by occupying the dogs brain, challenging it and creating positive outcomes for the dog to achieve, the dogs brain becomes better able to adapt and cope with the changes that life will inevitably throw at it. Equally a really good training session, where the dog is asked to work out solutions to problems, as you would create with shaping for example, will tire the dog out as much as a really long walk, when we pair these two things together, we have a very tired dog.

Environment

The environment in which the dog grows up is equally important. I would suggest that the key elements here are safety, security, and predictability. Has the dog got areas within the environment where it can feel safe, for example if the dog is in bed, is it allowed to lay there unmolested? is it allowed to choose where it sleeps? is the bed in an area away from the main group? so that the dog can sleep without fear of being knocked or bumped into. Are there raised areas for the dog to settle? It does not mean that dogs should be allowed on furniture but having dog beds which are raised up off the floor even only slightly, can help the dog feel more secure overall. Ideally a dog would be able to choose from a range of different sleeping areas without fear of being moved or told off. Predictability in both the environment and the actions and reactions of the people in it, help to reduce anxiety and reactivity overall. Put more simply the dog will quickly become accustomed to what is normal behaviour for the people it lives with, and so normality is the most predictable and reassuring state. Add into that a predictable routine, (though this can be quite loose) helps in the same effort. For example, if you feed the dog twice a day, then they should be fed roughly at the same time each day, though not precisely the same time, it would be good practice to vary feed times within half an hour of a set time. For example, if the dog is fed at 6pm, then some days it may get fed at 5.30pm and others at 6.30pm and any variation within that. This degree of flexibility allows for situations where you may be running late and unable to feed the dog at a set time.

Relationship

The relationships that we build with our dogs are generally specific to the individuals involved. It is certainly the case that dogs will dislike some individuals from time to time, equally, many people find that they like a certain individual dog, but do not quite 'gel' with another. How we then build relationships with our dogs, largely depends on the needs of the individuals involved. However, there are certain things that we can do to help build positive and creative relationships with the dogs that we live with.

Throughout this book we are looking at the different ways of helping build the relationship with our dogs, from the way that we train the dog, to the setup of the environment that we are asking the dog to live in.

If we can establish a solid relationship with our dogs, there are a number of beneficial consequences.

- The dog becomes keener to engage in activities with the owner such as training exercises.

- Attentiveness is more likely in situations where there are increased levels of distraction.

- Most importantly the dog's ability to recover from bad experiences is reduced and their ability to revert to normal is increased. For example, should the dog have a particularly bad experience at the vets, the presence of the owner can often help to reduce the overall impact of that event, allowing the dog to recover more quickly.

By taking the time to work on our relationships with our dogs we are more able to build the kind of lives which we are aiming for with them.

Given the individualistic nature of relationships it would be difficult to be very prescriptive in the way in which a person should go about building a solid one, however, there are a few things which we can do which will help to build a strong foundation for a more positive and rewarding relationship with our dogs.

Predictability - There is predictability in everything that we do, and when it comes to our dogs this predictability can be either a helpful thing, or the building blocks of some problematic behaviours. However, when it comes to building a relationship, predictability in our actions and reactions is necessary for the dogs to begin to understand our responses to certain situations.

We could also describe this as consistency, as owners we should attempt to be consistent in our own behaviours and actions allowing the dog to interpret these behaviours and associate them to a set of behaviours which they can understand. It is sometimes the case that we can be variable in our own behaviours due to our own stress levels, frustration, mood, and situation, and therefore these changes will directly affect the way our dogs perceive us. Sometimes our behaviour can be quite difficult to interpret, however, it is important that we remain consistent to ourselves, to be as normal as possible where our dogs are concerned. This means, for example, that if you as an owner are 'normally' quiet and quite reserved, you will notice the dog will react to you when you suddenly start shouting for whatever reason. The reverse is also true, that if you are usually a very loud outgoing individual, this is what the dog gets used to and these behaviours form the basis for the consistency and predictability of living with us.

Communication - this is a large word, as it is used quite widely and covers a myriad of different methods of interaction, from the communications between dogs, to how they then communicate with us, and how we communicate with them. At this point we are considering how we go about communicating with our dog. How do we explain to our dog what it is that we want from them? It is the methods that we choose here which can really help to build the relationships that we desire with our dogs. When considering the methods with which to communicate with our dogs we might think about the type of training we are going to use, the kinds of interactions that we want with them, whether they are ones of close contact or do we wish the dog to be slightly more at arm's length. Every interaction that we have with our dogs helps build the relationship, and subsequently the type of interaction dictates the type of relationship we end up with. To put this simply, how does the dog view us, do we herald positive interactions, or would the dog rather give us space. Does the dog run towards us when we appear, or satisfy itself with remaining where it is or even move away?

Training with our dogs goes a long way to building the kinds of relationships that we wish for. The more positive we can be with our training interactions, the more positive the relationship will be with our dogs.

Diet

Diet is essential for a happy, healthy dog; however, it is a bit of a minefield, and many owners find the decision as to what they should be feeding quite overwhelming. There are hundreds of different diets on the market, each with its own claim to why it is the best food for your dog. There are numerous groups on social media who will argue for and against certain types and brands of food. The best advice I have ever heard in regard to feeding, is 'feed the dog in front of you.' This basically means if the dog is showing signs of weight loss, weight gain, behavioural issues or loss of condition, if there are numerous small heath conditions constantly for no apparent reason, then change the diet, however, if the dog is doing well on that diet, they are maintaining a good weight, their bowel movements are nicely formed, they drink the appropriate amount and so on, then I would suggest it is the right food for that individual.

After that, one needs only consider whether it is financially viable to sustain the dog on that particular food.

In summary,

- Does your dog eat it?
- Is your dog doing well on it?
- Can you afford it?

If you can answer positively to the above questions, then chances are it is the right food for your dog. If there is any doubt, it is then worth chatting to your local veterinary surgery to see if they can help you work out a more suitable diet for your dog.

Health

Dogs can suffer a wide range of conditions which affect their general health and wellbeing. It is the role of the veterinary surgeon to be there to help you with your dog's health. It is only the vet which can diagnose and treat a condition, treating conditions without the vet can be dangerous and so registering with your local vet as soon as you get your dog is essential. For most owners, a trip to the vet is a fairly routine endeavor, and only occurs maybe once or twice a year, however, for some it can be a regular occurrence.

Finding a vet that you like, and trust therefore is important, as they will work closely with an owner to ensure that the dog is receiving the optimum care possible.

In all areas of animal care there are a number of measures that are used to assess an animal's quality of welfare, these measures are known as the five freedoms and have been universally accepted as the basic levels of welfare that any animal should have in order to be considered to be in a state of good welfare.

"In 1964, the United Kingdom developed the paradigm of 'Five Freedoms' in order to help the agriculture industry simplify welfare concepts, recognise the importance of wellbeing, and facilitate the adoption of adequate welfare standards." (Kleiman, Devra G, et al, 2010,)

The five freedoms are as follows.

1. Freedom from pain and injury and disease
2. Freedom from hunger and thirst

3. Freedom from discomfort
4. Freedom to express normal behaviours.
5. Freedom from fear and distress.

As far as the domestic dog is concerned it is generally accepted that the five freedoms are met quite easily, and for the vast majority of dogs in homes I would agree, however, there are some elements where they may not be quite hitting the mark. It is worth looking at them a little bit more closely to understand how they may affect the lives of our dogs every day.

1. I would suggest that number one is very well catered to for the majority of dogs, it is true that there are dogs which go for months without having injuries treated, or they may ever see the vet or receive medication for a particular condition, but thankfully these dogs remain in the minority and the majority of dogs receive treatment as soon as possible and are looked after in this way very well.
2. Again, for the vast majority of dogs freedom from hunger and thirst is well covered and most receive adequate food and have water readily available for whenever they want it.
3. Freedom from discomfort is where we start to get into quite grey territory, as an individual's tolerances for things such as heat and cold vary quite significantly. Certainly, the majority of dogs will be given a comfy bed to lie in, they will be allowed to lie on the floor and stretch out, however, one element that they have little control over is the central heating. For many dogs, the heat of the home is welcomed, and many enjoy lying in front of the fire or near a radiator, however there are many breeds where the ability to escape from the warmth is challenging. Breeds with heavier coats, breeds which are bred for more outdoors lifestyles, these breeds can find the heating of the home quite difficult as they

find it a challenge to find somewhere cool enough to be comfortable. Equally, dogs which live outside may require some greater level of heating through winter months to avoid being too cold. Being able to provide suitable temperature zones within a home is the optimum, it may be (as in my home) that one room, the living room, is kept at a comfortable temperature for people, whereas the rest of the house is kept slightly cooler, and the dogs are free to go between rooms in order to regulate their own temperature.

4. Freedom to express normal behaviours- here we run into a degree of uncertainty again, as it requires the ability to define what might be considered to be normal behaviours for a domestic dog. The answer to this depends upon how you are reaching your definition, for example if we compare the behaviours of domestic dogs and their wild cousins, then it becomes clear that there are a number of behaviours which they do not get access to, behaviours such as roaming over distances, the opportunity to breed (especially if they are neutered), hunting behaviours are limited. However, if we look at the domestic dog in its own right then 'normal behaviours' can be difficult to define, because the environments and situations which our dogs live in vary so considerably depending upon where they live and what is expected of them. If it is reasonable to conclude that if your dog is able to have a run around, play with other dogs from time to time, sniff as much as possible, urinate and toilet when needed, then it is achieving as many normal behaviours as possible, however, there is a degree of limitation imposed and if we were not in the equation are these all the behaviours that our dogs would choose to engage in, or would they opt for others. It is difficult to say conclusively, however, ensuring that we provide our dogs with as much opportunity to do

'doggy' things, especially with other dogs, goes a long way to ticking this box.

5. Freedom from fear and distress, this element is to ensure that no animal lives in a situation where they are scared or abused at the hands of their owners or handlers, unfortunately it is a fact that many dogs still undergo lives where they feel afraid to behave in ways which are appropriate for them. This could be due to the owner being particularly nasty to the dog, though this is again still in the minority, or it could be due to the environment that the dog lives in, a busy household, or in a cityscape with a lot of noise and hustle and bustle. Equally where we have dogs which are under-socialised, or poorly socialised then their ability to avoid fear and distress is much more difficult, even when they are living in a relatively normal situation.

I appreciate that this viewpoint is not necessarily shared by everyone, and in some respects, it is rather extreme, as the issues that have been raised are minor for the majority of the dogs which live with people have to experience, however, increasingly there is a kind of slow rot in the standards that we hold ourselves to when it comes to caring for our dogs. One of my own pet hates in animal care, is the use of clothing, I will concede that there are times when an extra layer may be required, breeds such as greyhounds surely benefit from a coat throughout the winter months and there are many other breeds where this would apply, however, increasingly it is common to see breeds with heavy coats wearing jackets on mild winters days, there are outfits which are designed to make the dog look like a teddy bear or something equally 'cute'. The problem here is that the acceptable viewpoint of how we consider our dogs gets slowly warped, causing them to slowly and increasingly become products and objects. These actions are often defended by stating that the dog feels the cold, or there is an aesthetic value which the owner feels enhances the dog's look. However, the overall effect is that the dog slowly becomes seen less as an individual and increasingly as another child or doll to dress up. Then when the dog attempts to behave as dogs should, they end up getting into trouble from the owner.

There are occasions where the use of certain types of jackets are quite appropriate as mentioned above, however, their use MUST be decided upon the need of the dog, and not by the desire of the owner to maintain a clean and unmuddied home, or for the aesthetic alone.

What is a dog?

The domestic dog is descended from wolves, there are many theories as to how the dog became domesticated and many thoughts as to the true origin species, though it is widely accepted that they are descended from *Canis Lupus*.

"Although contested in the past, the biological ancestry of the dog is now certain. On the basis of both genetic and behavioural studies the dog is a domestic wolf." (Lindsay, 2000)

Indeed, they share their genetic makeup with wolves, and consequently many comparisons have been made between wolves and dogs in order to try and understand the domestic dog's behaviour. Some of the advice that has come from these studies has been useful, whereas much of it has missed the mark in terms of explaining the behaviours we see on a daily basis. The way dogs and wolves' structure themselves differs slightly, and there are many differences between how they interact with the world. These differences are partly due to the way that the dogs have been raised, but also largely to do with the environment that they live in, namely the human one.

Further to this the domestic dog has been bred so intensively away from the original ancestor that they are hardly recognisable as being part of the same animal family, however, this does not prevent people from considering them as a little wolf in the home. Unfortunately, this can lead to a lot of misconceptions as to how our dogs will respond and react to many and all situations.

"*Many ethologists and zoologists choose to observe wolf groups living in captivity in order to gain a comprehensive description of their behaviour. Although the lack of detailed observations from the field made such investigations indispensable, there has, not surprisingly, been some disagreement about how this research should be interpreted.*

First, the captive wolves are often confined to a small space and have no chance to disperse over a larger area. Therefore, younger and/or submissive individuals are prevented from leaving the pack for shorter or longer periods in order to move out of sight of the more dominant companions. This could be problematic as the pack gets older, because under natural conditions wolves more than three years old leave the group" (Miklosi, Adam, 2015)

Understanding how wild canids organise themselves in terms of social structure can be informative for the purposes of trying to understand the origins of our dogs, however, this information can often influence our interpretation of the behaviours that we see, and it is necessary and important that we view our dogs in the context of where they live and how they interact with that environment, rather than seeking answers within species that are subjected to completely different influences.

Choosing a dog

Dogs have been bred successfully to fit in with our lives so much so that they could be considered a completely different animal to the wolf, the fact that they share the same genes with wolves becomes almost of little consequence in the way that we care for them or live with them on a daily basis.

Therefore, it would make sense to think of our dogs, not in terms of their ancestry, but more in terms of their breed, their family history (if known) and the environment within which they are going to be living, these are the factors that will most strongly influence the behaviours that you will see as an owner. Careful choice of breed is probably the first aspect that any owner will consider when they are thinking about getting a dog.

So, what are the factors which drive people to make the decisions on the type of breed that they end up choosing, put simply, they are many and varied, however it might be possible to break them down into certain types of decision-making process.

- The breed is known to the wider family - essentially, people will choose breeds which they have grown up with, for example if their mum and dad owned border collies, then there is a greater likelihood that the owner will want to have another border collie, however, it often the case that they do not necessarily appreciate the work involved as this was an aspect that they may never have seen their Mum and Dad undertake.

- The dog's looks - this is probably the next biggest driver in breed choice, which basically all boils down to the aesthetics of the breed. This may be something as simple as the owner considers the breed 'cute' and there are many dogs where it is clear that they are being bred for this element. It may be that the dog shares similarities with their ancestral cousins and have elements of the wolf about them. Or it might be that they have a physical presence which the owner likes. All in all, it is often the way that a dog looks that draws an owner toward that breed. Once the decision has been made to try and get that breed it is hoped that a new owner will then thoroughly research that breed and ensure that their lifestyle and experience is relevant to that particular type of dog. It is a reality that not all breeds suit all situations or experience levels. Some breeds require a little bit more understanding and knowledge before they are taken on, otherwise an owner can run into problems as the dog grows up.

• The source - Often owners will choose their dog based upon where they get them from. Whether the dog is from a breeder or from a rescue centre will dictate how much choice the owner has in terms of age and breed type. If an owner goes to a breeder there is a good chance that they will be able to see the dog's family history, they will have a good understanding of the dog's health status and the likelihood of the dog developing issues later on, though these things are never guaranteed. If an owner goes to rescue, the information that the rescue is able to provide will be limited by the amount of history that they have been given. They can only pass on the information provided by the previous home. If there is no history, then all they are able to tell an owner is how the dog is in the kennel environment. This information is useful as a guide to the dog's personality, but again is not comprehensive or dictatorial, as most of us do not live in a kennel environment. Therefore, taking on a rescue dog requires a level of commitment to the new dog which is slightly different to taking on a puppy from a breeder.

There are no right and wrong choices in terms of which breed or type of dog an owner decides upon, as long as the owner has done their homework and has understood everything that might be involved in taking on that particular type of dog.

When choosing to get a dog from a breeder, it is worth taking time, contacting a number of different breeders of the desired breed type, talking to them honestly about the situation, environment, and experience levels the owner has, and allowing them to guide the process as much as possible, as it usually the case that a breeder will understand that specific breeds needs better than most.

An owner should do as much homework as possible and make sure they are content that the breeder they are going to is legitimate. Many breeders will invite potential owners to meet the parent dog, sometimes before the pups are born, but more usually there will be a couple of meets before the puppy finally gets to come home. For many breeders, the homes where the puppies go become regular contacts as they receive updates on the puppies and act as a source of information should the owner have further questions once the puppy is home.

When doing initial research into the breed an owner should make themselves aware of how much it will actually cost for a puppy of that particular breed, most legitimate breeders will ask for a fee roughly the same amount, for example if a dog cost £1500 with one breeder, then the majority of genuine breeders will be charging roughly the same amount. Where puppies are advertised for far less than this then caution should be exercised as there are a number of ways that puppies are sold which do not come from legitimate caring breeders.

Equally if there is a reluctance to see the parent dog with the puppies, or the owner is being asked to attend an address where it is clear the puppies do not live, then caution. Often, the people selling from puppy farms will rent a house or a flat as a way to seem legitimate, often the new owner will be told that they have just moved in or are in the process of moving. Also being asked to meet in a car park to make the exchange is a warning sign that the puppy the owner is getting may not be from a legitimate or legal source.

The rescue dog.

Many of the rescue centres and organisations in the UK work hard to find their dogs suitable homes, and most are highly successful at getting the matches right, however, it takes a bit of compromise on the part of the new owner as well. The best way to walk into a rescue centre is with an open mind, as often the dog that is most suited to that person is nothing like they had in their minds eye when they began. Rescue and rehoming centres do not want dogs to come back and work very hard to make sure that a new owner walks away with the right dog for them, however, this is not an exact science, and the pairing can occasionally be incorrect, however, these amount for a small number of the overall rehomes that most organisations do.

It is also the case that most rescue centres will not have a wide variety of breeds, they may occasionally get the odd one or two, and in certain areas of the country you may find more examples of one breed than another, however, there is usually a dog there for most new owners. If there, isn't it is worth being patient as dogs come into rescue on a daily basis?

The following are a few tips to consider when deciding to go for a rescue dog.

- When you enter the rescue, centre try and be as open minded as possible regarding the type of dog that you are looking for. Often the most rewarding dogs are those which you have not previously considered.

- Take your time, if they have viewing kennels, take the time to get a feel for the dogs, often the right dog will 'speak' to you. A feeling you will get that the dog you are looking at is the right one.

- Listen to the rescue centre staff, they will know the dog well, and will advise you accordingly.

- Do not be too disappointed if the dog you like is not suitable for your situation, sometimes it will come down to something which may be beyond your control such as whether or not you live in a home with a garden or not. It is never a reflection on you as a person or potential dog owner.

• Be open to the suggestions of the rescue centre staff, they will be able to pair you with a dog which is best suited to your circumstances.

• Make sure that you visit regularly, the right dog will come along eventually, and when it does, it will be the best decision you have made.

• Rescue dogs rarely go home without a period of settling in, be prepared for this and allow the dog time to get to know its new situation. This will take work and depending on the dog some will need more work than others.

Rehoming is a hard job, and the rescue centre staff will always try and do the best by their dogs and by their clients, allow them to guide you through the process and remember to take your time.

Once you have found your new companion, avoid spending a lot of money on things such as luxury beds, plush toys and so on, keep things relatively basic until you have learned how the dog responds to the new environment, many owners become distressed when they find that their new companion has destroyed the dog bed which cost over £100, it damages the potential relationship. Once the dog has settled in a bit and you understand it a little better, then spend as much as you like on spoiling the dog. Contact a local vet and make sure you know what they need in order to register the dog, often they will want to meet the dog relatively soon after the dog comes home, this is usually just a meet and greet and a quick check over so that they are aware of any known health conditions.

Make sure you have suitable feed bowls, leads and toys for when the dog gets home, again keep these relatively basic until you know the dog well.

On collection day, listen to the advice being given by the rescue centre, they have developed their advice over many years of rehoming dogs, and they understand the potential pitfalls that may be ahead, they will give you as much help as they can, even once the dog is in your home.

Take the dog straight home, there will be plenty of time over the coming weeks to allow the dog to meet the rest of the extended family. On that first day, all they need to do is to get to their new home and investigate their new environment.

Make sure visitors are at an absolute minimum, a lot of people will be keen to come and meet the new arrival, however, the dog will be taking in a huge amount of information in a short period of time, they will also be full of the kennel environment, meaning that they will be potentially quite agitated, anxious, possibly fearful, therefore the quieter the first day is, the better. Make sure that the only people the dog meets on the first day are the people that the dog will be living with, allow it plenty of space to investigate the new home, and do not expect too much of it. The whole experience is very daunting for most dogs, and they will react and respond in a variety of ways, many of which can be quite unexpected.

Some of the most successful people to have rehomed a dog have simply taken the dog home and left it to its own devices. If the dog wished to interact then the owner responded, however, if it wished to hide in a corner and watch what was happening, then, that was fine too. There is plenty of time for the dog to learn the whole of its new life, the first day is simply orientation. It is sensible to make sure that on the first day home the dog is limited to the home only, do not attempt to take the dog a walk, owners who have a garden should stay within this area, if not then the dog should only go out long enough to evacuate its bladder and bowels, and avoid walking a long way from home.

Start as you mean to continue, therefore if the dog does things that you like, and you wish to promote, make sure you let the dog know that it did it correctly. Many people will give the dog a settling in period, where they will allow behaviours to develop which they do not want long term. This is slightly unfair as the dog will become used to the behaviours it learns in the settling in period and then suddenly the owner changes the criteria, effectively you are asking the dog to settle in all over again. Therefore, implement the routines that you want long term, from the first day that the dog is home, remembering to allow plenty of time and space for the dog to learn the new regime.

The dog is going to get things wrong, they will make mistakes, this is okay, as they will have never lived in your home before and therefore everything is new and they will be learning it all from scratch, be patient and guide them through what you expect of them, if they make a mistake, move on quickly so that they are given an opportunity to get it right.

Expect the dog to have no housetraining at all, it may be that the rescue centre told you that the dog has a history of being house trained or that they were clean in the kennel, this is good news as it means the dog is more likely to become house trained within the new home, however, the dog has never been house trained in your home, and therefore getting the dog out as often as possible to toilet will help the dog learn the new regime and increase the likelihood of the dog becoming clean more quickly. If there is no history of housetraining, then implement the same housetraining protocols as you would with a puppy, getting the dog out as often as possible and reinforcing the dog when it toilets in the correct place, and having no reaction to accidents in the home.

Give consideration to where the dog sleeps and expect a disturbed night. There are several options, I generally recommend that the new dog does not sleep with the owner on the first few nights, take time to find out whether or not the dog is comfortable sharing sleeping spaces, when dogs first come out of kennels, they may feel more secure without company. Make sure that the dog knows where you are but ensure that they cannot access the bedroom. The last thing a new owner wants is to wake up in the night to find a dog growling in their face because they moved in their sleep and the dog took offence. The dog is likely to make noise, calling you back, expect this and be prepared for a disturbed night's sleep. Avoid reinforcing this behaviour and if you need to attend to the dog, try and time your entrance into the room where it is when the dog is quiet, to avoid training it to bark inadvertently.

Over the coming days and weeks, it is possible to teach the dog to settle more effectively and it may be possible to move the dog towards a sleeping area closer to you, as you learn how well it copes with sleeping with company. This information is often gathered when an owner falls asleep on the couch on a weekend afternoon and wakes up to find the dog happily snoozing next to them. As the dog learns the new routines and regimes, then as an owner you can relax more and more, until the dog is living with you in a way which you and the dog are both comfortable with.

There are, understood settling in periods, or 'honeymoon periods. These are the periods of time that the dog takes to effectively rid itself of the kennel environment, and settle into its new home and routine, these periods are.

- 3 days = during this period the dog is still in the kennel mode, loosely we might expect to see two types of behaviour through this period, either quite fearful behaviour, where the dog seeks to avoid the new owners and hides away in areas of the home where they can simply take time to watch and learn. The other is where the dog has high levels of energy and the subsequent behaviours that are associated with this. Behaviours such as excessive chewing, over the top behaviours such as jumping up, higher levels of reactivity towards noises and sounds and so on.

- 3 weeks = During this period the dog is having to learn the new routines of the home and is still adjusting from the kennel environment. We might also expect to see prior learning manifesting itself, this means that if the dog has behaved a certain way in a previous home, we may see echoes of these behaviours starting to emerge when presented with the same or similar stimuli in the new home.

- 3 months = it is widely accepted that after three wells in the new home, the dog has settled, and the dog that the owner finds themselves with, is the dog that they will be living with for the rest of the dog's life. By this time the dog will have a good idea of the new routines, housetraining is likely to be under control or certainly on the right path, behaviours such as excessive chewing should be showing signs of diminishing, and dogs which were previously fearful, should be more comfortable interacting with all members of the household.

It is generally felt that after three months the dog has settled into the new home and that any unexpected behaviours should have made themselves apparent, and for the most part this is reasonably true, however, there is one final landmark and that is after a year. The reason for this is that it is unlikely that the dog will experience the full spectrum of home life in just three months, especially if the owner is taking their time in settling the dog in. There are other big life events which happen annually which can trigger unexpected responses in dogs, principally these are,
Birthdays

Christmas and New year

Halloween

Bonfire night

There are of course many smaller family celebrations which take place throughout the year, and all of these will have an effect on the dog. Therefore, it would be reasonable to suggest that a new owner only gets the complete picture of their new dog, once a full cycle of family events and regular occurrences takes place.

Given the above settling in periods, whether the owner takes their rescue dog along to training classes is a difficult one to give a general answer to as it will largely depend upon the dog and also the type of classes that the owner is considering going along to. Many dogs are highly reactive during the first three months, and it is natural for a new owner to seek help with getting on top of this behaviour, however, often a training class scenario may not be the most appropriate solution to this, as they are often in confined areas, with other dogs which are equally as excitable, and subsequently, the whole class descends into a lot of dogs all barking at each other. I have known many owners of rescue dogs asked to leave the training classes as their dog is too disruptive, which in itself is understandable, however, they are then often left high and dry without any advice on how to go forward with their dog to address the problem they went to the training class to address in the first place.

The best advice is to contact a number of trainers before the dog arrives in the home and seek their advice as to how best to approach this situation. Most trainers will be more than happy to work with you to try and get the dog into the classes in the most appropriate way, this may be introducing the dog slowly to the class, attending for short periods and building up. Larger training groups and classes may even be able to assign a trainer to help the owner integrate the dog in the most effective way. Smaller classes may offer a one-to-one session in order to build the dogs confidence at attending classes, whichever solution is decided upon, it is best to discuss it beforehand with the trainer so that everyone knows their role in the process. It is possible that the dog will attend the class without issue, but again the trainer will be able to advise on the best way to assess whether this is the case, before the dog attends and becomes a disruptive influence.

Whether an owner attends training classes or not, the new dog will require a degree of training in order to help it settle into the new home, it is unreasonable to expect the dog to know what to do the minute it arrives, therefore understanding the areas in which the dog would benefit from some training will really help the situation go more smoothly.

How dogs learn

Understanding how dogs learn things is fundamental to achieving success with our training.

Learning theory governs most of what we now understand as to the best way to train our dogs, even though the techniques in this book are widely proven to be the most effective and dog friendly methods, proven both in practice and in the laboratory, it remains that some people continue to use methods which cause fear and anxiety in their dog. It is hoped that once you have completed reading this book, and undertaken the exercises, you will find that you have trained your dog some of the basic behaviours, whilst having had fun.

The subject of learning theory is a very large one and can get rather complicated the further into you get.

Key terms

· *Operant conditioning – "is the part of the science of behaviour that explains the functional relationship between environmental events and behaviour. It is a key component in explaining how all organisms (including dogs) learn." (Burch and Bailey, 1999)*

· *Reinforcement – "occurs when a behaviour, followed by a consequent stimulus, is strengthened, or becomes more likely to occur again." (Burch and Bailey, 1999)*

· *Primary reinforcer – "are reinforcers that are related to biology. Examples of primary reinforcers include food, drink, some kinds of touch and sexual contact." (Burch and Bailey, 1999)*

Secondary Reinforcer - "are reinforcers that can be related to social conditions. In other words, they have a cultural context. Humans respond to secondary reinforcers such as praise, smiles, thumbs-up gestures, and money. Dogs are social creatures, and many dogs also respond well to smiles praise attention, clapping, toys and pats." (Burch and Bailey 1999)

· *Conditioned reinforcer- "A conditioned reinforcer is a previously neutral stimulus that begins to function as a reinforcer after being paired a number of times with an established reinforcer." (Burch and Bailey, 1999)*

Below is an example of how consequences can be divided into the four different types, two which involve adding and two involving removal.

Positive reinforcement – adding something to increase behaviour	**Positive punishment – adding something to decrease behaviour.**
Negative reinforcement -removing something to increase behaviour	**negative punishment – removing something to decrease behaviour.**

The most effective way of training is through the use of positive reinforcement. This means that we should only reward behaviours that we want, and that we should make sure the dog has every opportunity to choose the correct behaviour.

Even though as trainers we endeavor to work with our dogs primarily using positive reinforcement, that is of adding a 'something' likely to increase behaviour, it is important to be aware that the other elements of the table may also be at play throughout the training session. It is equally important to appreciate that the table does not necessarily reflect that the 'somethings' added or subtracted are either nasty or nice as perceived by the dog.

Dogs learn initially through trial and error – if the behaviour is reinforced, then the dog will repeat the behaviour. This is known as 'the law of effect' and was developed by Edward Lee Thorndike (1874-1949).

"Thorndike's Law of effect says response that produce rewards tend to increase in frequency" (Burch and Bailey, 1999)

Dogs learn constantly throughout their lives, much like we do ourselves. This means that they can learn behaviours which we do not want as easily as they can learn behaviours which we do want. The principles remain the same in that if we want to increase a certain behaviour then we must reinforce it consistently. If we want a behaviour to stop then we should endeavor to avoid reinforcing it as much as possible.

Reinforcement

What is meant by reinforcement?

Reinforcement is anything which increases a behaviour. Often these are things that the dog finds rewarding. This does not always mean that the consequence is something 'nice', just that it motivates the dog to repeat the behaviour. For example, it may be that telling a dog off for toileting in the house increases the likelihood of the behaviour repeating as the reaction of the owner is reinforcing, whereas no reaction by the owner would be more likely to decrease the behavior.

In general, as trainers, reinforcers are usually considered to be things which are 'nice' such as food, praise, and games.

The term reinforcer and reward are reasonably interchangeable, and either is appropriate. Sometimes it is easier to think of a reinforcer as a reward as this then means you are more likely to find something which the dog likes. It is important to remember that the reinforcer should be something that the dog really likes and not something that you, the owner, thinks it should like. For example, there is no point trying to reward good behaviour with a piece of cheese, if the dog does not like cheese. Therefore, taking some time to find out what your dog really likes is time very well spent.

Reinforcers can be graded as well, meaning that the value of the reinforcer to the dog should be established, which can then be used to let the dog know how well it has done. For example, for any new learning it is worth using something which the dog regards as high value, often this is something that the dog does not normally get such as chicken or sausage. Then once behaviours have been established, they can be reinforced with a lower value reinforcer such as a portion of the dog's breakfast or dinner.

Food is most commonly used as a reinforcer, as it is easy to give to the dog, it usually has a high motivation level, and it is easy to carry around with you. However, a reinforcer can be anything, such as a dog's favourite toy or game, or even simply a bit of appropriate attention.

Finally, it is possible to reinforce your dog through your own body language too, if you appear pleased with the dog's performance it is more likely to want to try and repeat the behaviour again. Smiling goes a long way with dogs, and therefore being happy about a dog's success will reinforce the behaviour too.

There are no hard and fast rules about what can be used as a reinforcer other than to say it should be easy to give and easily available. But most importantly it must be something that the dog likes and finds rewarding.

Conditioned reinforcers

Food, attention, playing games are all primary reinforcers, this means that they are naturally reinforcing to the dog, the dog requires them to survive and so will automatically achieve some degree of reinforcement from them. Conditioned reinforcers are things which the dog has learned to be reinforcing. These items will previously have been neutral, until the dog learns to associate them with a primary reinforcer. There are numerous examples of conditioned reinforcers and sometimes they can become problematic. One such example is the dog's lead, the association that the dog makes to the lead is that it means the dog is going to go for a walk, an opportunity to go for a walk and sniff and explore the environment. When the owner picks up the lead the dog performs behaviours, such as jumping about excitedly, which are triggered by the lead. Other common ones include, picking up car keys, the owner putting on a jacket or their shoes, and sometimes sounds can become conditioned if they are associated with a particular event or reinforcing circumstance, the car engine for example, even the theme tune to a favourite television programme.

"In clicker training, as in all conditioned reinforcement training, a reinforcer is paired with a neutral stimulus, and the neutral stimulus eventually becomes a conditioned reinforcer" (Burch and Bailey, 1999)

Dogs are able to learn that things are reinforcing very quickly, and often they have done so without us realising, however, we are also able to choose to teach the dog that certain items are reinforcing by pairing them with a primary reinforcer. The clicker is used in this way, by pairing the sound that the clicker makes with food, for example, the dog learns that when the clicker is heard, a primary reinforcer is on its way. This is often referred to as a bridge, as the sound bridges the gap between the behaviour and the delivery of the reinforcer. The reason that the clicker is so widely used in training, is that it is a very precise tool, and with practice and skill a trainer can reinforce extremely specific behaviours very accurately.

Once you have successfully conditioned the clicker, it is possible to start using it to train the dog with. There is sometimes confusion as to how the clicker should be used. The best way to think of it is as a marker of a good job. If you ask for a behaviour, such as a 'sit', click the dog for performing the behaviour, then follow up with the primary reinforcer.

"Reinforcement, extinction and punishment are three of the four basic principles of behaviour. These three principles are related to consequences that occur after behaviours. Reinforcers are consequences that strengthen behaviour; extinction and punishment are consequences that weaken behaviour. But to have a complete picture of behaviour, we must also understand the importance of antecedent events- the events that occur before a behaviour." (Burch and Bailey 1999)

This sequence is made easier through using the letters ABC. These stand for Antecedent, Behaviour, Consequence, when applied to the behaviour of sit, it may look like the following.

A = antecedent is the request to sit, either verbally or by hand signal

B = Behaviour, dog sits

C = consequence, dog receives the click, immediately followed by the primary reinforcer.

By following the above sequence, you are letting the dog know that the given behaviour was the correct one.

The Shaping game

(Taken from 'Don't shoot the dog' by Karen Pryor)
In order to improve your skills and particularly your timing with the clicker it is useful to be able to practice without the dog present. The shaping game is a good way of practicing without running the risk of teaching the dog something inappropriate. In order to play the game, you will need at least one other person, and a bowl of reinforcers.
The game is simple, it is basically a game of hot and cold, however it is used to help the trainer to better their skills as well as developing an understanding of how the learning process feels if you are the recipient.
To play the game, one person is designated the trainer, the other person is designated as the dog (the trainee). To start with, the dog should leave the training area, and the trainer decides on a suitable behaviour that they want the dog to do when they return. This could be something as simple as sitting on the couch, or more complex such as placing a particular ornament in a cupboard.
The dog
The task of the dog is to try and work out what behaviour the trainer is wanting. In order to achieve this the dog must come back into the room and attempt different things, this might be walking in a certain direction, attempting a certain behaviour, or even looking at a certain object or area of the room. When the dog hears a click, they need to remember what they were doing when they were clicked, then go to the trainer to receive their reinforcer. The dog's objective is to gain 'clicks' until the behaviour has been achieved.
The trainer
The trainer's job is to get the dog to perform the pre-decided behaviour. To begin with, keep behaviour simple, until you become more comfortable using the clicker.

The dog will enter the area and begin performing actions, the trainer needs to observe closely and click actions which let the dog know they are in the correct area. Think of it like a game of hot and cold, except that in this game the only indicator of being 'warm' is the click and if the dog is 'cold' then no click is forthcoming. Before you start it is worth breaking the behaviour down into approximations, for example if the idea is to get them to sit on the couch, then you can click when they walk towards the couch, however you can also click if they simply look at the couch. After each click the dog will return for a reinforcer. It is important that as the trainer you encourage the dog as much as possible, this means that you need to be clicking as regularly as you can. Long periods without clicking will result in the dog coming to a stop, unable to understand what is being asked of them. This means that as the trainer you will need to observe very closely for any behaviour that relates to the final behaviour and reinforce it.

The game is really useful to understand the importance of communication with the dog, when the only means of telling the dog they are doing well is the click, then it is important that the dog receives as much encouragement as possible.

Take turns swapping roles so that both participants experience how it feels in each role. Finally discuss with each other how you feel the session went, how it feels to be the dog when the only information was the click. It can be very enlightening, especially when there haven't been enough 'clicks'.

(Karen Pryor, 2002,)

Motivation

In order to motivate the dog during training we need to make sure that we are using reinforcers that are of the highest value, particularly when we are training something for the first time. The easiest way to think about this is to consider someone asking you to go to the shops for them, in return they will give you a bowl of cereal. You may consider it as you do like cereal, however, you eat it every morning and therefore when you are asked to do this favour, you decline, because the value of the reinforcer is not high enough to motivate you to do it, however, should you be offered £1,000.000 it is likely that you are out of the door and in the car heading to the shops, long before the request has been fully asked. The same apples to our dogs. If the only reinforcer that is on offer is a dog treat, then the motivation is going to be lower due to the fact that the dog gets something similar every day in their breakfast bowl. However, if the reinforcer available is something that the dog does not often get such as cheese, then the motivation to work with you is much stronger and subsequently the dog is much more likely to do the behaviour.

"To teach a dog a new behaviour, improve proficiency of a previously learned behaviour or maintain a behaviour, you must know how to use reinforcement effectively. that means understanding what kind of reinforcement is suitable in a particular training situation, and also knowing how and when to deliver that reinforcement. In operant conditioning, the rules pertaining to how many, or which specific responses will be reinforced are called schedules of reinforcement." (Burch and Bailey, 1999)

Just as with people, dogs are going to find different things reinforcing, therefore it is worthwhile not having any preconceptions as to what the dog is motivated by, for example if you were incredibly rich, but equally quite hungry, you may find cereal more reinforcing than the money.

When we are training, we need to keep the dog as motivated as possible, therefore using the most reinforcing item is a good idea.

When teaching a new behaviour, it is necessary to reinforce every time, as the behaviour becomes more established it is then possible to change how and when you reinforce, though it is essential that reinforcement is always given when you are asking for the behaviour.

For example, as the behaviour becomes more established you can place the dog onto a schedule of reinforcement which is random in nature, meaning that the dog is unable to predict when the reinforcer is going to be given, increasing the likelihood of the dog performing the behaviour reliably.

When reinforcing each behaviour every time, we are using a system of continuous reinforcement. This is an excellent method for training a new behaviour as it helps to establish a history of reinforcement, meaning that the dog learns that the reinforcement from the handler is reliable and constant. However, it is not good for ensuring the behaviour is solid, and is prone to extinction, where the behaviour tapers off when the reinforcers cease to be provided. One way to help prevent this is to move the dog onto a different schedule of reinforcement. As mentioned above, one of the most common schedules of reinforcement used is that of a variable ratio. This simply means that the delivery of the reinforcer in relation to the behaviour, varies unpredictably.

When reinforcement is delivered unpredictably, then the motivation to perform the behaviour increases, and the behaviour becomes much more solid and reliable. For the most part the variable schedule of reinforcement is the most used way of weaning the dog off of the continuous schedule, however there are a number of other schedules at an owner's disposal, depending upon the desired outcome, all the schedules are as follows.

- Continuous reinforcement

- Fixed ratio - this is where the reinforcer is delivered after a predetermined number of repetitions of the behaviour.

- Fixed interval - this is where the reinforcer is delivered after a predetermined amount of time has elapsed.

• Variable ratio - where the reinforcer is delivered in an unpredictable number of repetitions of the behaviour.

• Variable interval - where the reinforcer is delivered after a varied amount of time has elapsed.

The effective use of reinforcement schedules helps to ensure that the desired behaviours are reliable and consistently implemented. It is also the case that when undesired behaviours have been established, the inadvertent use of reinforcement schedules is clearly evident.

Most owners will instinctively use both continuous reinforcement as well as variable ratio reinforcement, without much consideration to its application, however, it is worthwhile taking the time to understand how the method of reinforcement affects the dog's behaviour, in order to ensure that we get the most out of our dogs.

Choice and control

The ability for the dog to be able to have control in its own training is important both for the welfare of the dog as well as the success of any given training session. The easiest way to think about this would be to consider the lessons taken in school. Those lessons which were engaging and where the teacher would create an environment where the learner was able to be active in their own learning, were usually retained by the learner more readily, whereas lessons which were monotonous and boring, where the teacher simply rattled off the information as a list, without engaging the learner, this lesson was usually forgotten reasonably quickly, and more importantly, the learners enthusiasm for attending the lesson would be significantly less.

The same can be said for training with our dogs. Sessions which are repetitive and boring, edged with consequence and where the dog feels that they are under duress in some way, will be much less successful than sessions where the dog is allowed to engage with the training or not.

Put simply at the beginning of every session, invite the dog to take part, if the dog declines, then accept this and attempt the session again at a later stage. Equally if the dog declines or shies away from the session midway, then allow the dog to take a moment and then invite them back in, if they decline then try again later.

How do we invite the dog to take part?

Usually when we train, we will undertake a number of ritualistic behaviours, these may be taking the treat pouch from a certain cupboard, fetching the clicker or other piece of training equipment, also the way that we stand, approach the dog, even down to the clothes that we wear are all cues to the dog that a training session is about to occur. Mostly your dog is likely to get excited at the prospect of training, for the chance to work for his or her favourite treats, however, occasionally, the dog may decide that it wishes to remain where it is or may even indicate that it wants to move to a different room or even the garden. In reality, after working with your dog you will very quickly appreciate the subtle behaviours which tell you that the dog is not wanting to engage at that particular point. The important aspect in this is to pay attention to what the dog is telling you and adapt your training plan or session to suit.

By training when the dog wants to learn you will find that the dog learns more quickly, and your relationship with the dog will go from strength to strength.

Of course, this principle does not just apply to the training sessions, it can be implemented and adopted in all interactions that we have with our dogs. The most basic activity that we engage in, is that of stroking or petting our dogs. It is often the case that the dog may not want to be petted at that particular time, however, it has learned to tolerate this attention, and therefore the owner does not pick up on the subtle signs that the dog is uncomfortable. However, if we as owners learn to tune into these subtleties then we can teach our dogs that they can choose when any interaction takes place.

This is different from dogs which constantly pester for attention, these dogs are controlling interactions for a number of reasons. It relates more towards dogs which are otherwise settled and engaged in calm behaviours; however, they are then subjected to the owner's attention regardless of whether they wanted it or not.

The relationship where the dog is comfortable with choosing its own interactions often begins when the dog is just a puppy, however, it can start at any time. As owners we simply need to be more aware of the dog's subtle behaviours when we wish to interact.

To keep it simple, if you wish to have a cuddle with your dog, invite them to join you, if they do, then begin by petting the dog as normal, then after a count of five, remove your hand and wait and see what the dog chooses to do. If the dog steps forward and instigates further interaction then it is clear that the dog wishes for the interaction to continue, however, should the dog attempt to move away, then he or she should be allowed to do so. The interaction can be invited again later, it is just at this particular moment, the dog would rather do something else.

You might even find that after lifting your hand from the dog, the dog actually repositions itself so that you end up petting the dog at some other point on its body, such as its rump.

This process encourages the dog to interact with you in such a way that communication between owner and dog is strengthened which only goes to help with the process of training and living with your dog.

Of the dogs that have shared my life, one stands out as a particularly good teacher of this premise. His name was Tawney, and he was a Saluki cross. His history was unknown and had come to live with via a rescue centre. For the most part he was a very affectionate dog and settled in well with us and the other dogs that we had. However, it became clear early on, that he appreciated his own space. He would growl and snap if anyone ever approached his bed, or if he thought they were going to, regardless of their actual intent, it was his perception of what was happening which would trigger the behaviour. For the most part this caused little issue, as it was quickly established that his sleeping areas were set up out of the way of traffic areas, and everyone learned that if Tawney were in his bed, he could be invited out, but if he did not want to then he would be left well alone. This system worked well, and he soon relaxed into family life, knowing that he had control of this aspect of his life.

His need to be able to control interactions with people was not limited to his sleeping area, however. Like most dogs he would often approach for a fuss, if you were sitting in a chair, he would place his head in your lap and appear to want to be petted. This would be tolerated for a short while, then he would freeze, and if you were not aware that he had done so, this would be followed by a snap, he would never make contact, but he would slink away, clearly unhappy about the interaction. However, should you stop fussing with him when he froze, he would back away, turn around and move his butt towards you so that he could get some butt rubs. He would usually tolerate this for much longer and clearly enjoyed this interaction. Also due to the fact that he was facing away from you he could move away at any point he chose.

He taught us very quickly that through paying close attention to the dog's behaviour during interactions, relationships between owners and their dogs can significantly improve.

It is also a particularly useful tool when it comes to children and dogs, as it is important for the dog to be able to feel confident enough to indicate to the owner that it is uncomfortable, this means that the owner can then intervene in the interaction and ensure that the dog is able to gain the space that it needs. By monitoring interactions between children and dogs, and sometimes even adults, it is possible to help both parties build strong, reliable relationships with each other, and minimizes the risk of any incidents which may result in damage to either party.

Equally, when we intervene between children and dogs, we are more able to teach the child how to look for the relevant signals from the dog which let them know that the dog is not happy with what they are doing.

The idea of choice underpins much of the training that we undertake with our dogs. For example if we are teaching heelwork, we set up the situation so that the dog positions itself suitably enough to be able to receive the reinforcer, the next time that the dog is presented with the same cues, it has a choice, when it makes the desired choice, then once again it receives the reinforcement, however, should it not choose as the owner desires, the owner simply sets up the situation again so that the dog can make the desired choice.

Fight, Flight, Freeze

"When confronted with aversive situations, dogs typically cope by engaging in activities that serve to reduce the danger:

Escape from eliciting stimulus (flee)
Displace the source of aversive stimulation (fight)
Increase vigilance or searching behaviour (flirt)
Wait for situation to change (freeze)
Tolerate or accept the situation (forbear)." (Lindsay, 2005)

Fight, flight, and freeze are important behavioural cues which the dog provides us to indicate a state of arousal at the time. They are linked to the dog's threat response and are designed specifically to prepare the dog for whichever outcome is most appropriate. The terms are fairly self-explanatory and are usually listed the opposite way around to how the dog will use them. For example, upon facing a threat initially, the dog will freeze, this can be brief in duration, a couple of milliseconds, but it will be there, or it can be prolonged and obvious. The freeze is the body's automatic response to the threat, and it is at this point that the dog is making decisions as to its next move. As a general rule, most animals will opt for flight where at all possible. This means that they move away from the perceived threat and get themselves to a place of safety, this is usually the preferred option as it is the one which will result in their continued survival, getting into a fight is always a risk as there is always the chance the animal will become injured, which is the last thing that they want. If flight is not an option, then they will fall back to the last resort which is to fight their way out of trouble.

Fight is a word which evokes images of dogs engaged in a brawl of some description, however, it can equally refer to a dog which has bitten. Essentially it has used a level of force in order to repel the perceived threat.

What is a threat? The important aspect of this question is not what is the threat? What does the dog think of as a threat? This is an important distinction, as the things that we may consider as perfectly normal and reasonable behaviours, can often be seen as potentially threatening to the dog, this in turn then triggers the dog to go into a fight, flight, freeze response. For the majority of small incidences where there is a perceived threat, the dog seldom moves into anything more than an a set of alert behaviours, ears up, watching and so on, maybe the dog might move position, maybe even move through to a different room, and then the incident is over and done with, this might be because the dog found the way a person entered a room a bit too much, or they were too loud and so on. It may be that a person has approached with unclear intentions and therefore the dog will move away without any incident. However, where the perceived threat is prolonged, as in the person keeps coming, and the dogs' options for moving away from the person are limited or nonexistent then the dog may opt for defending its position with a growl, or a more threatening set of behaviours, if this still does not work then the dog will resort to more aggressive vocalizations and possibly even a bite. As far as the person is concerned, they had done nothing wrong as they were just trying to say hello or sit next to the dog, and they essentially missed all of the dog's subtle cues to let them know to calm down or back off.

The freeze behaviour is one of the most useful cues to inform us of how our dogs might be feeling about a situation. The behaviour is often brief, and people can miss it easily, however, it is the behaviour which can cause a physical response in ourselves. When people first start in kennels, working with hundreds of dogs from various and often unknown backgrounds, they are taught never to ignore the little voice in the pit of their stomachs, that uneasy or uncertain feeling which comes from somewhere and lets you know that something is not right. It might be that if asked, the person would not be able to tell you exactly what was wrong, but they just knew that something is not as it should be. This is our response to the sometimes-imperceptible cues that the dog is giving us that tells us they are not comfortable with the actions that we are taking. Kennel staff were taught never to ignore that feeling and to follow it without analyzing it, as it was sometimes the difference between leaving the kennel unscathed or getting bitten.

It is difficult as with a different member of staff the dog may be perfectly fine, and on another day at a different time the dog causes no concern for that particular individual. But, in that instance at that time, the dog was not comfortable and was letting that individual know.

When we listen to that little voice, we are more able to diffuse potentially reactive situations before they develop further. Equally, the dog learns that as a person they are more able to communicate effectively with you and it goes a long way to helping build a solid relationship.

Failing our ability to pick up on freeze behaviours, then the freeze option is one which we should actively encourage in our dogs. If they appear to look uncomfortable and they wish to move, then creating a situation where they are able to move away helps to further diffuse the situation and build relations.

It is often the case that once the dog learns that it is free to move away from things that concern it, they will often choose to remain, it is the knowledge of an option that helps them to feel comfortable enough to remain within a situation which they may have at one time felt they needed to escape from.

If we as owners are more tuned into the freeze and flight responses, then we can more effectively avoid the fight response.

The difference between the owner's ideas of what is threatening and what the dog perceives as threatening, can lead the situation to escalate, as the owner is not necessarily prepared for a fight response in the situation that they are in. This in turn can lead to a bite occurring, seemingly without warning, however when the behaviour is analyzed it becomes clear that many of the subtle levels such as freeze were missed or ignored.

The other effect of the fight, flight freeze response is that the dog's body, in preparation for the next move, begins to generate a number of different hormones, including adrenaline and cortisol. all of which are designed to allow the dog to respond very quickly.

Fight, flight, freeze is generally referred to as the three F's, and most people will understand what they stand for, however, there is a fourth F which is not commonly talked about, this is mainly due to the fact that for many years it was not necessarily understood to be part of the threat response. The fourth F is known by a number of different terms, all beginning with F, but it is often best to think about the behaviour as 'Fiddle about'.

Fiddle about behaviours are behaviours which are seemingly out of place or context for the situation. They are called displacement behaviours and occur when the dog is otherwise unsure of how to behave in the situation. Many people will find them odd when they see them, and you will often hear owners refer to their dog as being 'silly' or 'thick' as the behaviour appears to be so out of context, however, these behaviours are useful little indicators as to how the dog is perceiving the situation, and how much the dog is coping with what is being asked of it. If ignored, then these behaviours can flow into the fight flight freeze responses as the dog feels under pressure by the owner or the situation.

It is worthwhile, when spotting displacement behaviours, to take a moment and assess the situation to try and understand what might be happening that is causing the dog confusion or concern. For example, in a training session it is not uncommon to see displacement behaviours occurring whenever the criterion for the task is changed or moved on. The dog becomes quite comfortable with the level of training, and then the moment we begin to make the task a bit harder, the dog becomes a bit more confused and therefore begins offering behaviours which appear to be out of context. It is at this point that the trainer should revert back to a task that the dog is more comfortable with and commit to taking the transition to the new criteria a little bit slower, or it may be possible to break the task down so that the dog is only being asked to make little steps forward. By doing this we can help avoid an increase in anxious behaviours as well as avoiding the dog shutting down completely where it is unable to partake of the training at all.

It is not only in training scenarios where we can find displacement behaviours, they can happen whenever the dog feels a bit confused or more specifically unsure of what to do. As owners these are a set of behaviours which we should tune into as a way of further understanding how our dogs view their particular world.

Equipment

The equipment that we choose to use with our dogs, whether we are training or not, is important as each piece of equipment has a particular use and purpose. It is necessary to know how each item works and how it affects the dog as this will help to ensure the best results in our training. There are many variations of things such as leads, collars and harnesses, and it is important to choose the right ones for yourself and for your budget. This section is designed to give you a basic understanding of the form and function of the equipment so that you can make the best choice available to you.

Collars

Collars are the most common piece of equipment to be found on a dog and are particularly useful in many circumstances, however, they are equally open to abuse, therefore it is important to make sure we are using the right type of collar and using it correctly. Dogs are not born with the knowledge of wearing anything about their body, placing any piece of equipment on a dog requires a level of training and adjustment. Collars are usually the first piece of equipment that is placed upon a dog and often it is done so abruptly and without any time for the puppy to adjust. It is important that time is taken to teach the puppy to accept the collar, by associating the collar to happy, pleasant things such as attention, or food. Keep the introductions short, building up the duration of time that the puppy has the collar on, until the pup is eventually wearing it comfortably.

There are a number of different types of collars, the most common are known as flat collars, made out of nylon webbing and of various sizes, you can also find rolled collars, similar to flat collars, just a different style. Notably, certain breeds will have collars specifically designed for them, greyhounds for example have a particular shaped collar which is designed in such a way that it cannot slip off over their heads. This is because their neck is larger than their skull, allowing a standard collar to simply slip off.

Other collars of note are slip collars, check chains, and half checks. We will look at these in more detail further on.

Collars are usually used as the point of attachment for the dog's lead, however, for many dogs this can cause them to choke as they pull into the lead, potentially causing damage to their throats and their ability to breath properly later on in life. If a dog is to be walked using its collar it is a necessity that they learn to walk on a loose lead. Otherwise, they act as an easy and convenient location for identification tags.

Leads

Flat leads – most useful and versatile piece of equipment and most common. regularly standard 3 to 4ft in length, however 6ft training leads offer the most variability for most owners as they have double clips to help with attachments.

Chain leads - these are usually quite short, often no longer than a standard three-foot lead, this is largely due to the weight that would be created if they were much longer. They are useful for use with dogs which habitually chew through fabric or leather leads, however, they should be viewed as temporary until the training to overcome the chewing behaviour is implemented. Equally, due to the uncomfortable nature of the chain lead, many dogs will jump higher to grab the handle, and usually the owner's hand at the same time.

Harness – most useful piece of equipment for walking a dog as it offers most comfort to both dog and to the owner, helps control the dogs centre of balance and gives the dog the chance to exhibit normal greeting behaviours. Helps the dog feel more secure in the environment. When choosing a harness, it is important to ensure that it is fitted correctly and is comfortable for the dog to walk in. There are numerous styles of harness and not all of them will suit all dog types, therefore finding the correct harness and getting it fitted correctly is time very well spent. Most pet shops are able to help with fitting the harness, and there are numerous fitting guides available online. It is best to buy the best quality harness that you can afford and ensure that it has plenty of soft padding, especially around the areas which are under high levels of movement, such as the tops of the legs etc. Harnesses will not stop your dog from pulling, this is a behaviour which requires training; however, they do help a lot in making the process more comfortable for both the dog and the handler.

Stop go harness = works by applying pressure underneath dogs front legs – limited use, mainly useful as a temporary solution with a dog which pulls excessively, and all other avenues have proved fruitless. down sides can make the dog feel more insecure and has the ability to damage and injure the dog

Head collars = useful for dogs which require another level of control. especially useful with dogs which have aggression issues, not good for dogs which pull excessively into them, or which are behaving in an anxious or worried manner. can cause long term damage if used or fitted incorrectly.

Long lines = incredibly versatile piece of equipment, can teach loose lead and recall effectively, also provides an increased level of control whilst out on walks. Dogs and owners require practice in order to use them most effectively.

Check chains, prong collars etc., all have specific purposes and are not required or necessary in teaching loose lead or recall. These pieces of equipment are designed to work through the use of discomfort, for example should the dog pull excessively then the collar tightens and causes the dog discomfort. However, like all things they require training. A check chain, is designed to be checked a couple of times early in the training, causing the dog to associate the sound of the chain chinking with pain and discomfort, causing the dog to self-correct its behaviour, however, too often it is possible to witness dogs pulling into the check chain, causing them to have laboured breathing and subsequent damage to the throat and neck. These pieces of equipment, though readily available, should not need to be used by every owner and should only ever be used by an experienced professional, though they should only ever be a last resort and are seldom required when the appropriate training has been put in place.

Loose lead

When we talk about loose lead, we are simply talking about a dog which walks on lead with no tension present. The clasp which attaches the lead to the collar, or the harness should be loose and without tension. We are not necessarily referring to heelwork, which is a quite different discipline, however, it starts with loose lead.

Why train loose lead?

First and foremost, it makes walking the dog much more pleasant and enjoyable for the owner as the dog is not constantly dragging the owner wherever it wants to go. The dog is able to make much better choices as it is more able to take the time to make decisions when faced with something new such as another dog or a stranger approaching.

Overall, the dog is more relaxed, and this significantly reduces the likelihood of the dog reacting badly to other dogs. The majority of reactive dogs tend to also pull heavily on their leads. This upsets the dog's centre of balance and subsequently builds a degree of anxiety in them when they are walking. Effectively putting them on alert when they should be enjoying a sniff here and there.

When dogs pull on the lead it shifts their centre of balance, causing them to lean forward, as if they are in a perpetual state of falling over. This in turn, increases their levels of arousal so that they then become much more aware of their surroundings. Equally, if they are walking on a collar, then the collar and lead will raise the dogs head so that they are less able to perform normal greeting behaviours such as sniffing, further increasing the likelihood of reactive encounters.

The combination of these factors leads the dog to remain in a higher state of arousal than if there were no tension in the lead and if the dog was not pulling excessively.

Heelwork and loose lead are similar however, with heelwork we are asking the dog to walk next to us in a specific position, whereas with loose lead we are simply asking the dog to walk without any tension in the lead. This also means that the dog has a degree of freedom to move about and sniff and investigate the environment it is walking in.

There are a number of ways to teach loose lead.

· Be a tree = this method is simple as all it involves is as soon as the dog places any tension in the lead, the handler stops and stands still until the dog removes the tension itself, either by returning to the handler or simply stopping and relaxing. At this point the dog receives reinforcement. This method is slow, and at the start the handler will often not get far on their walk. Also, sometimes the distraction of the environment can be too much for the dog to focus on the training.

· Turnabout = this method is similar to 'be a tree', except that instead of stopping, the handler turns and walks in the other direction, again reinforcing the dog for walking in the correct position. This method is once again, quite slow and the owner is at risk of losing interest as the progress on a walk is slow, often the owner may not even reach the end of their street during the early stages of this method. Therefore, it is not one that produces reliable results in the real world.

· Follow me = This method can be highly effective. To teach the follow me, we begin by walking the dog in one direction, then just before the dog reaches the end of the lead, turn, and start walking in a different direction. The turn should be about 90 degrees. In order to avoid jerking the dog on the end of the lead, it is important to teach the dog to look at you when you say the words 'this way'. To do this, reinforce the dog every time you say it and then turn in the new direction. Very quickly the dog will learn to watch your every move and as a result will keep close to you when out walking.

· Next to me = this method is closer to teaching heelwork in as much as we are asking the dog to be in a certain position directly next to us. When the dog is in position, we simply make sure we reinforce it with a treat. Though we are asking the dog to be next to us in this exercise, it is up to the owner/ handler, where the dog actually ends up in relation to them. The important part is that the dog is not pulling on the lead and that there is no tension in the lead at all. This method is the preferred method as it is the most likely to achieve a satisfactory result, by using a clicker to mark the position as well, this method can be trained very quickly to a relatively high standard.

With all the above methods, it is important to make sure that you begin teaching them in quiet areas with few distractions, and build slowly into areas of greater distraction, only moving forward in the training once the dog has mastered the previous environment.

These are only a few methods that are possible to try, the one thing they all have in common is that they are asking the dog to check in with the handler. This is important as the dog needs to feel that the handler is more interesting and exciting than the environment that it is walking in.

The same is true for the next exercise – recall.

Recall

Recall is a simple behaviour to ask of the dog, but one of the most difficult to establish consistently in all environments. However, it is an essential behaviour if you wish to let your dog off lead in any public space.

The world is a busy place, and it is not always easy to know who is around the next corner, your dog may be the nicest dog in the world, however, the next dog you meet may not be, therefore the ability to get your dog to come to you when you need them to is particularly important.

Put simply, recall is asking the dog to come to wherever you are, from wherever it is. This can be a distance of a couple of hundred metres, to only a few feet, it does not matter as the behaviour is exactly the same in both cases.

The important thing about recall is that the dog wants to come to you. Therefore, it is essential that the dog is rewarded EVERY time it comes back to you. To begin with, use high value reinforcers such as the dogs favourite treat, as the dog gets better at the behaviour the value of the treats can reduce. But make sure that the dog is always reinforced for the behaviour.

There are times when the dog may ignore the initial command due to having met another dog, it is all too common to see an embarrassed owner telling the dog off when it finally recalls, this is detrimental to the training as the next time the dog is much less likely to come back when called.

There are no shortcuts with recall, the only way to improve it is to make sure you practice, then when you feel you have practiced enough, practice some more in every environment you can think of.

Safety tips

Walking dogs in public spaces has its own challenges, and things can happen that spook your dog, or distract them when you least expect it. Therefore, some simple safety tips are advisable.

· If in doubt, don't' – this specifically refers to letting your dog off lead. If you are unsure of the area, maybe it is the first time you walked there, keep your dog on lead until you know that the dog is settled into the area.

· Always walk your dog on lead near a road. It does not matter how well trained your dog is, roads and streets are increasingly busy, and anything can happen to spook your dog.

If your dog is off-lead and you are approaching another dog, bring your dog back under control and close to you until it can be established that the other owner is happy for the dogs to meet. This is necessary as you do not always know what the other dog is like, and the owner may be working hard to train with it or build its confidence.

The subtle art of walking a dog.

This title seems to be a little bit unnecessary in many ways, as the typical response is 'well how hard can it be?'. In many ways this is a reasonable reply and in truth, walking a dog is not that difficult at all, you apply the lead, and step out into the world to enjoy the sights and sounds and enjoy the great outdoors. That is the dream at least. However, there are many other elements that should be considered when taking your dog out of the house.

Time of day. Obviously, some points of the day are going to be a lot busier with people and dog walkers than they will be at others. It is worth thinking to yourself whether the time you are taking the dog for a walk fits with your routine, or with the dog's needs. Many times, a dog's reactivity, for example, can be reduced by simply changing the time of day that it is taken for a walk.

Where do you walk the dog? Is it a case of needing to walk the dog around a busy inner-city park, or is there suitable access to the countryside and the open hills? Is there a beach nearby? Are the local areas safe to walk at all times of the day? Is the dog better to be put in the car and driven to a more suitable area to go for a walk? Unfortunately, not everywhere is dog friendly and there are some environments where dogs would be unwelcome. Many local authorities have by laws in regard to exercising dogs, whether they can be let off lead or whether they have to be kept on, does the area have a large wildlife population, will the walk take the owner near to livestock, and so on, the list is fairly endless. But these are questions which should be considered.

One fundamental question which owners often fail to ask themselves is 'are you willing to pick up poop, then carry it with you until you reach a suitable bin?' It seems that the obvious answer should be 'yes of course' however, there are many dog owners who are unwilling to pick up the poop, and if they do then they do not wish to carry it around with them and leave it in situ in a bag for everyone to see. Equally perplexing are the dog walkers who pick up the poop, and then hang it in a tree! I would presume that the owner places it there with the intention of collecting it on their return, however, something happens that redirects their journey, or they simply forget. Whatever the reason this practice should not be started in the first place as it is unpleasant for the people who eventually have to clear up the area, and it gives all dog owners a bad reputation. The message is simple, if you are not prepared to clean up after your dog properly (which means taking it away with you) then do not get a dog.

Walk to you and your dog's capabilities, by this I simply mean if your dog is unable to walk great distances, or the owner is unsteady on their feet for whatever reason, then a cross country ramble may not be the most sensible. A dog's fitness levels fluctuate the same as ours do, therefore there may be times when a cross country ramble is appropriate, whereas at other times it is the worst kind of walk you could do. As dogs get older, their exercise needs change equally, it might be that they do not change significantly, but it might be that they run or walk a little slower, they might find it more difficult to tackle uneven surfaces and so on. Owners will also have spells of illness or times when they do not wish to take the dog for an exceedingly long walk, this is also fine, as long as the dog is quite content to have either a reduced walk, or even as far as the odd day at home, without going for a walk at all. One of my dogs enjoys her walks for the most part, however, she would much prefer to stay on the couch watching daytime tv, she is quite happy to go where she is required. My other one, is getting older and struggles to manage the distances he did in his youth; therefore, we go for shorter walks more often, these now tend to be just long enough for them to evacuate their bowels and bladder and have a good sniff so that they can catch up on all the latest news from the park.

Dog walking is great exercise, it is a good way of getting out into the world, getting fresh air and finding the joy in the little things, however, the world is increasingly busy, the number of people with dogs seems to be getting more and more, and when once upon a time you could walk the dog in an area and not see another person, increasingly dog walking is negotiating joggers, other walkers and other dog walkers. This means that we need to be prepared for the unexpected whenever we step out the door with our dogs.

One of the fundamental elements to walking a dog is being aware of the environment around us, if we are more attune to what is happening then we are better prepared for dealing with the unforeseen. There are some simple steps that we can take as dog owners to help mitigate when things going awry.

1. Leave your phone in your pocket. The vast majority of owners which I see when out walking my dogs are on their phone in some way or another, it may be that they are staring at them, or they may be involved in a call, either way, being on the phone takes the owners attention away from the actions and behaviour of the dog that they are walking. I have been in situations where I have been dealing with a wayward dog, intent on picking a fight with mine, all the while the other owner is busy on their phone, when they finally engage with the situation, they are often unapologetic and seem to feel that the problem derives from the fact that I was in the wrong place at the wrong time. If as owners, we ditched the phone (do not leave it at home as it is a useful form of communication should something go really wrong) but leave it in the pocket. Then it frees up a lot more opportunities for us to interact with and engage our dogs with learning good behaviours when dealing with events in the environment

2. Keep your dog on lead as a default. This is not to say that dogs should never be off lead, I am a great advocate of the dogs ability to free run and enjoy the environment in the way that they should, however, the areas where dogs can legitimately get off lead are on the decline, this may be because of the sheer number of other dogs, the need of other groups of people to use the area, the locality in relation to others species of animals and so on. The judgement as to whether or not to let the dog off is on the owner at the time, and each occasion that the owner finds themselves in that area, then the judgement needs to be made specific to that time. For example, just because the dog free ran in that area yesterday, may not mean it is appropriate today. If in doubt, keep the dog on lead.

3. If your dog is off lead, then be aware of dogs on lead. This is

more important now than it has ever been as dogs on lead
will be so for a reason. This could be that they are elderly,
maybe they cannot see very well, perhaps they are recovering
from an operation, more often than not they may be reactive,
scared, fearful or even sometimes aggressive. The number of
times that I have dealt with owners of a reactive dog who have
been abused by other dog walkers because their dog is
aggressive is depressing, especially when upon analyzing the
event it turns out that the reactive dog was working so hard
to be under control, whereas the 'nice' dog was constantly
baiting it, by running in, and running away, allowing the dog
on lead no chance to communicate effectively or deal with
the situation in an appropriate way. Often it is the owner
with the dog on lead who ends up feeling as though they are
in the wrong, whereas it is in fact the owner with the dog off
lead that should have brought their dog under control and
allowed the other dog to pass without incident.

4. Be aware of other species, when we are out walking, we are
    walking in their world, often times, especially in urban areas
    wildlife becomes accustomed to the presence of people and
    the element of fearful reaction is dulled, a deer in a park may
    see hundreds of dogs a day, therefore the one that attacks it
    may not have triggered as an effective flight response than if
    the deer was more aware of the potential dangers. When
    walking in areas where there is wildlife, keep your dog close
    by, avoid allowing it to roam too far, and if wildlife is obvious,
    put the dog on lead to avoid the chance of an incident which
    is traumatic to all involved.

5. When walking in the countryside, make sure you are aware of
    the rules involved with walking in that area, in some parts of
    the UK it is ok to roam where you want to as long as you
    follow the countryside code, keeping your dog on lead closing

gates behind you, taking your rubbish with you etc., in other parts of the UK it is not acceptable to roam where you want to. Make sure you know what the rules are in the area that you are walking, especially if you are walking in an area which is not your normal local area.

6. Livestock - Livestock offer a particular challenge for many dog walkers as many dogs retain a strong predatory instinct, which can often be broken down into an eye, stalk, and chase motivation. For a lot of dogs if the other animal remains still, then the chase instinct is not triggered, for others the mere sight of another animal triggers a chase reflex. Livestock are not able to deal very well with a dog running loose among them, especially the small species such as sheep, even if the dog has no intention of harming them, even the simple act of chasing them around is enough to cause irreparable harm as they become scared and risk cardiac arrest, for ewes which are in lamb then the risk of losing the lamb is significantly high. Irrespective of the financial and emotional impact upon the farmer, the effect that this event has upon the flock is significant. For larger livestock such as cattle, there is the added risk to the dog itself, cows are quite good at banding together and will often give chase to a wayward dog, and on occasion injuring the dog quite severely. All of this can be avoided by the owner by simply paying attention to where they are walking, making sure their dog is kept on lead and allowing livestock a good amount of space. The same is true of horses, though often horses will come close to us as they ride past. Again, it is a case of making sure that the dog is kept under suitable control. My greyhound really dislikes horses, he is fine if they are in a field, he will simply ignore them, however, if they are out with their rider, then he will bark excessively and generally cause bother, therefore we walk in

areas where we are unlikely to encounter horses, and if we are in an area where we may happen across horses, then it is a case of as soon as a horse is spotted we will turn around and walk in a different direction.

7. Finally, it is worth mentioning that an owner should only walk as many dogs as they can control. Increasingly, there are owners out with multiple dogs, and it is difficult to guarantee control over a larger number of dogs, and it is likely that they are perfectly lovely dogs, however, the dog that they meet may not be so friendly and as a result incident can occur. If an owner has multiple dogs, then split walks may be something to be considered until such a point that they have suitable control of them in the majority of situations.

Walking dogs is not therefore as straightforward as simply walking out in the world. It is a case of being very aware of yourself and your dog, as well as what is happening in the environment. Everyone wants to be able to enjoy their walks with their dogs, and if we all applied a little common sense to the walks then we can make everywhere a pleasant walking experience for all.

There is another aspect to walking a dog which all dog owners must be aware of, and that is the legal duty that all owners have when they are out in the world with their dog. There are a few laws which affect dog ownership, however, the most significant one is the Dangerous Dogs Act 1991.

"*The Dangerous Dogs Act 1991 did two main things:*

1. *It made it a criminal offence for the owner and/or the person in charge of the dog to allow a dog to be 'dangerously out of control' in a public place or be in a place where it is not permitted to be. As a result, if a dog injures a person, it may be seized by the police. Penalties can include a prison sentence and/or a ban on keeping dogs. There is also an automatic presumption that the*

dog involved will be destroyed (unless the owner can persuade the court that it is not a danger to the public, in which case it may be subject to a control order). The owner may also have to pay a fine, compensation and/or costs.

2. *It banned specific types of dogs include the Pit Bull Terrier, the Fila Brasiliero, the Dogo Argentino and the Japanese Tosa. Any dogs of these types were subject to a mandatory destruction order" (Anon, 2021, Kennel Club website online, available at https://www.thekennelclub.org.uk/about-us/campaigns/dangerous-dogs-deed-not-breed/, accessed 21/6/2021)*

Most people have heard of this piece of legislation, however, very few realize that it actually impacts all dog owners, most people only think that it applies to certain breeds only. This is not the case, and all dog owners can find themselves on the wrong side of this Act if they are not paying sufficient attention.

Most famously Section 1 of the Dangerous Dogs Act places restrictions upon the ownership of certain breeds, these breeds are.

1. Japanese Tosa
2. Fila Brasiliero
3. Dogo de Argentino, and
4. American Pit Bull terriers

Unfortunately, there is a great deal of variation within the definition of the American Pit bull and subsequently many are seized and then it has to be proven that they are not in any way a Pit Bull. For the most part, owners will look at their dog, and given that their dog is not one of these breeds will pay no further attention to the Dangerous Dogs Act, however, it is important to be aware of section 3.

Section 3 states that a dog is deemed dangerous if it is "found to be dangerously out of control in a public place or makes someone think they may get bitten". This statement is all encompassing, because a dog dangerously out of control would be a dog with no control. An owner who is constantly calling their dog, only to find that it is happily ignoring them whilst it bounds across the park towards another dog would be technically in breach of the law, if their dog subsequently caused an injury, or made the other person feel that they were going to be bitten.

Section 3 applies to ALL dogs, whether it is a Labrador or a chihuahua, and any owner can find themselves in breach of this law. In order to stay safe, following simple common-sense steps will help to make sure that everyone enjoys their walks safely.

Housetraining

Housetraining is the process of teaching a dog to remain clean in the house. This training is most commonly associated with puppies; however, dogs of any age can require housetraining. Once again as with many training activities there are no shortcuts to success.

Dogs are not naturally mindful of waiting to go to the toilet and so we need to teach them. there are key times when a dog will need the toilet, these are.

· Upon waking up.

· After eating and drinking.

· After playing.

· And often after a walk – this is because the world can be an intimidating place causing the dog to be uncomfortable toileting in unknown areas, therefore access to the garden upon return is prudent.

Whenever your dog meets one of the above criteria, you need to take the dog out. It does not matter what the weather is like, you will need to remain with dog in the garden until it has toileted. It is then really important that you reward the dog for doing so. Make sure that the reward is of high value and that the dog gets a positive message about how excited you are that they went to the toilet outside. Make sure to take the dog out at the above times, and then also randomly at points throughout the day.

Throughout the house-training process, the dog will have accidents in the home. How you handle these events is so important as to whether your training succeeds or fails.

It is necessary to make sure that you do not reinforce the dog for having an accident in the house. All too often it is the owner's reaction to the accident which can be the reinforcing element. If we consider the following scenario, we should be able to see how reinforcement can inadvertently train the dog to toilet in the home.

Let us say the dog sleeps in a room downstairs whilst the owners sleep upstairs. The dog has always toileted through the night even though the owners have been diligent in following the appropriate advice for toilet training. However, when the owner comes down in the morning, they consistently tell the dog off for having the accident through the night.

In this scenario the dog has effectively been ignored for the whole night, and consequently the reaction of the owner, even though it is negative, is enough to associate the act of toileting with getting attention. Further to this it is more likely that the dog learns to expect a telling off first thing in the morning that the anticipation of this is enough to cause the dog to toilet.

The best reaction to accidents in the home is no reaction at all, instead greet the dog normally as if they had not had an accident, remove the dog from the room and get on with cleaning up the mess.

The best way to clean is to use a biological detergent as these break down the enzymes in the toilet and once it has been cleaned away, is less likely to leave a scent in the same place encouraging the dog to toilet there again in the future. If the accident is on carpet, then make sure that the detergent is allowed enough time to soak through to the underlay. Then allow the area to dry before letting the dog back into the area.

Many things can affect housetraining, so patience is essential, and dogs can lose their house training at any time during their lives, especially if they have moved to a new house or been frightened and so on. If your dog does lose its housetraining, simply revert back to the original training process and they should quickly adapt to the new circumstances.

Socialisation

Socialisation and habituation are two aspects of raising a dog which are possibly the most important elements that any owner should focus on. In terms of when this should be done there are some key times in the dog's development where they are most open to the process of understanding the world around them, however this process is ongoing and therefore consideration should be given to how we introduce our dogs to new things.

When beginning to take your dog out into the world, it is worthwhile considering the environment itself. The dog's ability to retain information is compromised with the greater levels of distraction that are present in a busy environment. To help with understanding how best to train your dog with distraction, it is worth thinking of the environment in terms of traffic lights.

Red areas are those areas which have the greatest degree of distraction in them. They are places which are busy, either with people or other dogs, but equally they may simply be areas which the dog finds rather challenging, this may be near to a school, or next to a busy road. Red areas are the ones which cause the dog's brain to fill up with other things, reducing their ability to focus on the task in hand such as walking on a loose lead. Generally, once identified, red areas should either be avoided, or moved through as quickly as possible until the dog has reached an area which is much less intimidating.

Amber areas are those which have high levels of distraction, however, they are not as intimidating or challenging as red areas. These may be busy areas, which the dog has become used to and consequently the environment is slightly more predictable. It is still a challenge for the dog to concentrate in amber areas, and any work taking place in an amber should be brief in nature, with the majority of the work taking place in green areas, with only brief excursions into amber.

Green areas are those with the least amount of distraction, they are often areas where the dog feels comfortable, they are familiar and predictable. In these areas the dog's ability to focus on training is at its greatest and therefore it is green areas which allow for new training exercises to take hold.

Once a behaviour has been trained in a green area, reliably, then the training can begin to move into increasingly amber areas, subsequently turning them green. As the dog progresses with the process amber areas turn green, red areas turn amber and so on.

The trick is to avoid training in red areas, as no learning will occur. The best solution, once a red area has been identified, is to move through it as quickly as possible and get to an amber or green area, only then should training be attempted.

It is possible to apply the traffic light system to all aspects of the dog's life and environment, with assessments on the relevant colour being made through close observation of the dogs' reactions to the specific areas in question. For example, if it is a struggle to gain the dogs attention, then it is likely that the area where the training is being attempted is either amber or red.

The most obvious area to apply this idea would be for the dogs' regular walks, allocating the various different areas with the relevant colour so as to most effectively implement the training. However, it is also likely that the home environment itself is filled with micro areas of red and amber and subsequently affecting the training in these areas too.

For example, the living room may well be a green area, where the dog has few distractions and is happy to engage in training exercises successfully, however, the hall and front door might actually be amber or even red as the association of excitement overcomes the dog's ability to concentrate. This means that the trainer needs to account for this and build behaviours from the living room out into the hallway and towards the front door.

It is also necessary to not assume the colours of given areas. It might be that we would consider the garden as a green area, as there is only the dog and the household which use it. However, consideration needs to be given to the wider environment beyond. Where it may be that we as owners are unaware of the wider distractions, our dogs on the other hand will be very in tune with them, from the sounds of people walking past the garden, to barking dogs, traffic, children playing and any number of other environmental stimuli. All of this impact and potentially cause an area such as the garden to become amber. Finally, a behavioural history in the specific area will also affect how well the dog engages with the learning process. For example, if the dog has always been told off when on the couch, there is the potential that being in the living room, with a certain individual is enough to impede the dog's ability to learn.

When we consider our environment in these terms, we are more able to set up each training session so that it becomes the most effective and successful session possible.

What is socialisation?

"We want to raise puppies that can well in our society. What we are aiming to achieve can be described as: 'an active process of teaching a dog how to behave in all situations, through pleasant experiences.'" (Appleby, et al, 2016)

Socialisation is the term given to the process of exposing our dogs to the greater world. This includes people, dogs, other animals, traffic as well as everyday things such as vacuum cleaners and washing machines. All of these things when first experienced present a possible challenge as each has the potential to be very scary to our young dogs. It is our job therefore to make sure that each time the dog experiences something new, it is done in the most positive way possible. Dogs have critical developmental periods, and it is advised that socialisation should be done with puppies between the ages of 4 weeks to 6 months, basically as soon as the puppies open their eyes, they can process the world around them effectively. However, given that most owners get their puppies at 8 weeks or older, then there is a need to get on with socialising as much as possible. To begin with, getting them used to the environment they live in is the most obvious starting point, allowing them to explore their surroundings and making sure that they receive nice experiences around things such as family members and everyday items such as vacuum cleaners and washing machines.

How to socialise

As puppies grow, they take much of their information regarding what is scary and what is not, from the reactions and behaviours of other members of their group, specifically the reaction of the mother. Generally, for things which are of little or no concern, non-threatening objects or situations, the mother will continue as normal, barely showing a reaction, this then shows the pup that the thing is of little concern. The mother is careful not to reinforce any worried or anxious behaviours that the puppy may have shown. However, if the situation is deemed to be threatening, then the mother reacts accordingly, often gathering the puppies to her and defending them. This is an important point to remember as we can accidentally reinforce worried and anxious behaviour without meaning to. It is also important to remember to expose your dog to new things at a pace that your dog can cope with. If we throw them in at the deep end too quickly then they can easily become overwhelmed and instead of seeing new experiences as positive, they can develop behaviours designed to create space and make the new thing go away. One of the most common is the use of aggression towards new people or other dogs. Much better to have a plan of building the dog's confidence slowly and making sure that each experience is positive.

Each new experience requires management, the young dogs as yet are not necessarily equipped to make the right choices and as a consequence it is important that we create positive and reinforcing experiences.

People

People present one of the biggest challenges when it comes to socialisation. Young dogs have expectations of interactions, they find it difficult to be ignored and will often try and interact with people in inappropriate ways such as jumping up and mouthing. We can prevent some of these behaviours by firstly introducing to people that we already know and trust and have an input in how they interact with our dogs. We want people who understand that the dog needs interaction, but equally space to control the interaction. People who are overly friendly with the dog, can cause the dog to become worried and respond by growling or snapping. Young children are particularly guilty of this as they find it difficult to read the subtle signals that dogs give out.

When exposing the pup to strangers it is useful to have the puppy focus on you for the most part. They can say hello to people that you as the owner feel will interact in an appropriate manner. It is possible to use the dogs' favourite treats in order to build confidence in the situation.

Remember to reinforce calm confident behaviour, avoid reinforcing worried or anxious behaviours, if you see any signs of anxiety, then the best solution is to change the situation to one that the dog coped with previously, by either changing the dog's position, or creating space between you and the other person.

Build up the puppy's exposure slowly, start by walking in quiet areas, and move into more busy areas as long as the pup is showing signs of enjoying the experience.

We need to make sure that the pups are introduced to as many different people as is reasonable to do, we need to make sure that every conceivable type of person is included in the list of people that we want our pups to meet. For most owners it is easy enough to find a varied amount of people within their own group of family and friends, it is necessary however, to look at this group closely and ensure that the puppy gets introduced to people who are quite different to those in our close social groups. For example, if the family unit has a Mum and a Dad, with two young children, the owner needs to make sure that the puppy is introduced to teenagers and older people, also people with pushchairs, walking sticks, tall people, short people, long hair, short hair, and so the list goes on. Also, it is important to realize that exposure to a couple of members of each group may feel sufficient, it is important to make sure the puppy is introduced to as many individuals within this group as possible.

It is the case that when we are introducing people, the best way is to try and do it in a passive way. This means that the puppy gets to watch people going about their normal business, without them necessarily attempting to interact with the puppy. Good places for this type of socialising would be finding a quiet corner in a cafe or a pub which allows dogs in, and simply quietly sitting, allowing the puppy to observe everything going on, whilst making sure it is reinforced for nice calm, relaxed behaviour.

For young puppies, those which are still to be fully vaccinated, it is still possible to undertake an effective socialisation process, instead of allowing the puppy to walk by itself, the owner would simply carry the puppy, and allow it to absorb the environment passively. It is important to keep these sessions short, but frequent so as to avoid overloading the puppy's brain with too much information all at once.

Other dogs

Other dogs pose unique challenges when we are socialising young dogs. It is important to allow them to meet as many different dogs as is reasonably possible, having said that any dog that you choose to introduce to your young dog have to be as well balanced as possible. Letting the pup meet randomly in the park will more often than not create situations in which the pup can end up being bullied or worse.

Introducing your pup to known dogs, or carefully structured introductions at a training class are the best way to start.

Once again, we are looking for nice calm, enjoyable interactions between the dogs, with regular interruptions whenever play gets too much or too rough. Once you have met a few dogs, you can start building the dog's confidence with other dogs out and about.

Off lead. Whilst you are building the dog's confidence it is worthwhile maintaining your pup on a lead. This way you can control the interactions more closely and ensure that each interaction is positive and enjoyable.

Try and ensure that the puppy meets as wide a range of other dogs as you can, as only mixing the dog with dogs of its own age will limit the amount of social learning that the puppy will receive. It can be difficult to meet other dogs which are suitable but walking in the park will usually offer suitable opportunities. It is important though to make sure that there is communication between the owners so that everyone is happy for the interaction to take place. If another owner is reluctant or hesitant, it is important to respect their wishes and not allow the puppy to interact with their dog.

For the most part other owners are usually quite happy to allow interactions to take place, and all too often they will happily talk about their dog and the puppy, whilst the two dog's play.

One of the more common issues owners face when walking their dogs is the situation where another dog owner allows their dog to come up and interact without first checking whether this interaction was wanted. Often this is a dog off lead, pestering a dog on lead, and subsequently this can lead to a number of problematic incidents.

If possible, it is helpful to try and create space for the dog on lead, by dropping the lead and allowing the dog the space to appropriately deal with the interloper, however, this is not always possible and so trying to keep the lead as slack as possible will help. As soon as it is practical, attempt to get the other dog under control, and then it may be possible to continue the interaction at a more appropriate pace for both dogs involved.

Sometimes these interactions can lead to a situation where the puppy becomes scared or intimidated by the other dog. If this happens it is necessary to move out of that particular situation, and calm the puppy down, however, it should not stop other meetings and interactions taking place as it is important that the puppy learns that it was an isolated incident and for the most part meeting other dogs is an enjoyable and happy experience.

Communication

"On a most basic level, communication can be defined as the reciprocal exchange of information between two or more individuals." (Lindsay, 2000)

Dogs use many techniques to communicate, some are verbal, some are scent based, but most are visual. They use all parts of their body to communicate emotions or intentions. As a species we are not particularly good at picking up on many of the signals that our dogs give us, however, dogs are particularly good at reading our body language this leads to a degree of miscommunication in many of the interactions that we have with our dogs. Many of the dogs' communication behaviours can be very subtle and are often easily overlooked by owners and handlers. Dogs will use these subtle behaviours to attempt to let us know when they feel uncomfortable, or frustrated, confused and so on, however, when they are missed or overlooked, the dog will then move to more overt indicators such as body postures and vocalisations. We can use these subtle behaviours to help inform the progress of our training sessions as the dog will use many of these signals to let us know when we are moving too quickly or when the dog is getting bored and distracted. Many of the more well-known signals are as follows.

> Yawning - When dogs yawn, many owners simply assume that their dog is tired, however, it is worthwhile looking at the points in the day or the events that are taking place whenever the dog yawns, as it is often the case that the dog is yawning by way of attempting to calm a situation down. Yawning is a behaviour used by many species as a way of stating that they are not a threat, and this is also true of dogs. Often dogs will yawn when a particular person enters a

room, or when something is happening in the environment which they feel uncomfortable with.

Lip licking - this behaviour is much more subtle than a yawn as it can often get overlooked, however it often indicates the same intention from the dog. One where the dog is attempting to indicate a level of discomfort to the owner.

Averting a gaze - when dogs look away from us in an obvious attempt to avoid staring or engaging in prolonged eye contact. This is another behaviour which dogs use to attempt to reduce conflict and tension within a situation.

Jumping up - this behaviour is most commonly associated with situations where the dog is overexcited and often when they are happy to see the owner after arriving home. However, it is also a behaviour which is often seen when a dog feels uncomfortable with a situation or environment. It appears slightly different as the dog will often be looking at the person or object that is causing it concern at the same time as they are jumping up.

● Prolonged stretches - body posturing is a quite common method of canine communication, with a wide range of postures used, including the use of stretching. Dogs will often use a prolonged stretch to help calm an approaching individual and indicate that they are friendly and would be open to play. These prolonged stretches look similar to a play bow; however, their meaning is slightly different. With a play bow, the intention is to engage the other dog in a game, they are often brief in nature, and look more like a bounce than anything else. When this posture is held for any length of time then the meaning changes to one of attempting to calm the situation.

The number of signals that dog use to communicate with us is extensive and often we will miss or overlook them, however, by paying attention during a training session we are more able to pick up on these signals and adjust our training session accordingly.

In her book *'Aggression in Dogs, Practical Management, prevention and Behaviour Modification'*, Brenda Aloff identifies five categories of signaling in dogs, which are used specifically for conflict resolution.

1. *"Stress-related topography (observable behaviour, behaviour sequence, or physical reaction) is that which is primarily reflexive – the physiological symptoms of stress.*

2. *Displacement Signals are behaviours done 'in place of' something else and are specifically out of context. The dog may be using a familiar activity to 'comfort' herself. These signals indicate to others that the dog is feeling stressed.*

3. *Calming Signals are used as a way to avoid threats and to communicate a wish to prevent confrontation. The dog uses these signals both to calm himself and to communicate to others nearby that he wishes them to remain calm also. These signs indicate that the using them has an awareness of personal space infringement (either his own or the other dog's), and he wishes to communicate his own non-aggressive intent or good will.*

4. *Distance Increasing Signals (from your dog's point of view), which say, 'please move out of my personal space,' or perhaps, 'Move right on out of my territory.' Maybe even, 'Move right on out of my life.'*

5. *Distance Decreasing Signals are an invitation from a dog to approach. A Yielding behaviour would be one type of Distance Decreasing Signal. A Yielding behaviour is something the dog accesses to appease or to turn off or prevent aggression in another dog or human. Another Distance Decreasing Signal would be a play bow or a paw-lift, both of which are friendly overtures inviting one to 'come hither' "(Aloff, 2002)*

Communication is key to any relationship whether it is with a friend, a work colleague, family member or our dog. Successful relationships tend to be based on excellent communication.

· Dogs mainly communicate visually through body posture, eye position and so on. Approximately 75 % of canine communication is visual, with only a small portion being based in verbalizations.

· Conversely humans are much more verbally communicative, with only a small element being based in visual communication.

· Dogs have adapted over time to be able to read human body language very accurately.

· We have failed to do the same.

Key points in canine communication

Due to the vast array of body postures and subtle body positioning, to cover all aspects of canine communication is too large to cover in a simple book such as this, however there are some key points which we can highlight and use as a foundation to help us understand much of the other behavioural indicators that we regularly see.

Dogs use communication much the same as we do and that is to indicate intent, whether this is the intention to play, mate, aggress or any other reason which requires interaction with another individual. When dogs are happy, we as their owners often find them quite easy to read and understand, for example a play bow. This is used to encourage another individual to enter into an appropriate game, however it can also be used for informing another individual to calm down or to give an individual space. When signals are used in this way, we generally refer to them as calming signals.

"Calming Signals are studied extensively by Turid Rugaas. (Her book, On Talking terms with dogs: Calming Signals, is a must read.) They are used specifically and deliberately by a dog to 'calm' down others in the environment" (Aloff, 2002)

Calming signals range from behaviours such as

- Ear position
- Eye position
- Tail position
- Yawning
- Lip licking
- Play bow (held for a period of time)
- Averting eyes.
- Turning head.
- Posturing the body away.

These behaviours in the past have often been interpreted as submissive, however they have a much more subtle function than that as they are designed to calm the interaction between two individuals, they are often subtle and often get overlooked by owners and handlers. They are designed in some way to create space in an interaction, to buy time and to change the dynamics of the interaction so that it is more conducive to both participants.

Calming signals are low level behaviours designed to change the behaviour of another, if they are ignored or overlooked then the dog may well resort to more intense signals to get their message across. Given the choice the dog would usually opt to move away when calming signals get ignored, however this is not always possible (especially in a home environment) and so the dog will feel as though it has little choice other than to resort to behaviours which are a little clearer, such as a growl or a bark at the offending individual.

Fear responses

When individuals feel threatened, they undergo a biological response. This response is known as Fight, Flight, Freeze, and is designed to enable the individual the chance to assess a threat and opt for the most appropriate course of action in order to survive. It is a very primal reaction and one that is not under conscious control.

Fight = this is fairly straightforward as the dog feels that the only way to defend itself is through overt aggression, such as a bite

Flight = again simply the dog will run away (however, sometimes this behaviour can be as subtle as moving away slightly)

Freeze = this one often gets overlooked as the dog will simply remain where it is and stop moving. This can be incredibly brief before the dog resorts to a fight response due to perceiving no other option.

All of the above reactions ready the body to act in support of its own survival. The body releases adrenaline, noradrenaline, and dopamine in readiness, each one of these hormones enables the dog to react much more quickly and can provide pleasant sensations in the recipient (a reason why some people become addicted to extreme sports etc.). At low levels dogs will use calming signals to try and calm a perceived threat, therefore they are good indicators of a dog's general emotional state.

There is a fourth response which a dog will use to a perceived threat and that is to 'Fiddle about' This is any behaviour which does not fit into the context of the situation. An example of this would be if you were to ask a dog to lie down and it continually gave you the ball. It is also often a sign of confusion with a request or a situation.

It is important that whenever you see any of the above behaviours that you take a minute to assess the possible problem and endeavor to change the situation. This could be as simple as changing your own position in relation to the dog, or leaving entirely, however reacting in a considered, slow manner will usually relieve the situation.

Finally, we want our dogs to understand that we will listen to them whenever they try to communicate with us, for the most part we will miss the majority of the subtle behaviours such as calming signals, but regularly react to the more obvious communications such as growling. It is important that we respond to a growl by acknowledging it and not chastising the dog for growling, this way we can encourage the dog to use it as a suitable communication method, rather than learning that it does not get listened to when they are uncomfortable, as the consequence of this is that the dog simply resorts to going to the fight (bite) response and this is what we want to avoid.

In the above descriptions I have referred to a 'perceived threat'. This is because actions or incidents which we feel may be fairly innocuous, may actually be fairly intimidating and threatening to a dog. An example of this may be the dog which likes to sleep on the owner's couch in their absence. The couch is a unique thing as it offers the dog an incredibly safe space to relax whenever they are feeling innerved, or anxious, often this is seen in dogs which are new to a home, or dogs which are already scared and worried such as when fireworks or thunder are occurring. The couch is high up off the ground, protected on three sides and the bonus is that it is really comfortable, an obvious choice for a nervous dog. If we then go and try and move the dog from the couch by taking hold of its collar, it is not unreasonable for the dog to feel that it is being threatened unduly and subsequently resort to growling or worse, biting the owner. Therefore, we can use calming signals and other communicative signals to help us interpret the dog's emotional state at any given time and therefore inform us of the most effective and appropriate action to take next.

Calming signals are also incredibly useful when we are training as the dog will often use them to let us know when they are struggling with a concept or when they have had enough of the training, meaning that we can therefore tailor our training sessions so that the dog always feels comfortable during training.

One problem that many owners have is overcoming our own preconceived ideas of how our dogs should behave and interact with us.

There are as many different theories on how dogs organise themselves socially as there are researchers and behaviourists studying it. However, it is increasingly agreed that the one way that dogs do not organise themselves is through the use of a linear hierarchy.

For many years it was thought that dogs and their wild counterparts would follow a social structure which was linear in nature, meaning that the group was led by an alpha animal and all other individuals fell into line beneath them.

"In recent years researchers have revised the social model of the wolf pack. The earlier model was based on a behaviourally enforced strict linear hierarchy. This model assumed that all wolves aim for the dominant position because this is the only way to ensure the propagation of their genes, This view was changed on the basis of field observations which showed that most packs raise only a single litter, pack members belong to the same family, and young wolves leave the pack between one and three years of age (Gese and Mech, 1991, Packard, 2003)." (Miklosi, 2016)

This is so entrenched in our own social psyche, that much of human literature and even our own business and workplace structures follow the same model. The uses of words such as 'Alpha', 'Dominant', 'Submissive' are used easily when people are talking about dog behaviour, however, this model does not, and has never stood up to scrutiny. When looking at the social structure of wolves for example, it is clear that the 'pack' is a family unit, with Mum and Dad, raising their offspring and teaching them how to survive in the world as a wolf. As the young wolves grow, they separate off and move away, with the view to forming their own family 'pack'. Within the family group, resources are often assigned to those that need them most, this could be for various reasons including age and ill health. The main aim of the wolf family is to ensure the survival of all of its members. This means that if we were to assume that dogs follow a similar social structure, then it stands to reason that the way they are attempting to communicate with us is through a need for mutual cooperation to access the resources it requires to survive and thrive. When we look at dogs with this viewpoint, then many of the behaviours we see on a day-to-day basis start to make a bit more sense, than if we assign the linear hierarchical model.

"The 'hierarchy' and the 'family' models have many common elements. However, while the former model refers to wolves as 'alpha, beta,....omega animals' or 'dominants' and 'subordinates', the family model prefers categories such as 'leaders' or 'breeders'. This propagation of new categories has created some confusion in the literature, and it would be useful to settle for one unified nomenclature. In any case, however, these changes in our understanding of the wolf social system should be also a warning for those who apply these concepts uncritically to dogs." (Miklosi, 2016)

To summarise, as owners our role is to help our dogs navigate the world in which they live and to help them thrive and survive appropriately. This is done through a combination of methods including, exercise, socialisation, training, health care and a safe home environment.

Problem Behaviours

Problem behaviours range in type and intensity and more often than not they are only really problems due to the owner's perception or expectation of how the dog should be behaving, when we take a step back and look at events from the dog's point of view, the behaviours usually make a bit more sense and therefore, the solution can sometimes present itself quite logically. There are many problem behaviours that have significant effects on the dog's welfare, and this section is not designed to be a how to guide in problem solving, therefore if you have any concerns over your dog's behaviour it is best to get in touch with a trainer or behaviourist in order to get an accurate assessment of the behaviour and subsequently the correct advice. It is also important that when dealing with problem behaviours you avoid seeking solutions via the internet or television, as more often than not the advice given is generic and may not necessarily apply to your dog's particular situation.

Many problem behaviours that trainers and behaviourists encounter, have been practiced over a long period of time, before the owner feels it necessary to get in touch, by this point they are looking for quick fixes as both the stress levels of the owner and the dogs are at breaking point, unfortunately, most long term behaviours require quite involved, often long term solutions, with behaviours that make up aggression often requiring significant changes to the owners daily routine and lifestyle. Therefore, it is best to seek advice as early on as possible in order to ensure that any behaviour modification programme can have its maximum efficacy.

Particularly in the case of aggressive behaviours it is best to get advice from a professional at the earliest opportunity, aggression cases are often complex, and require multiple skill sets to resolve, including management, training, and veterinary inputs. Therefore, it is not in the remit of this text to look at aggression other than to give a suggestion as to the most common types that owners may experience.

The first thing to consider when we are thinking about behaviour is that it does not occur in a vacuum, meaning that in order for a behaviour to take place, it requires a functional outcome for the individual displaying the behaviour. It is possible that the true nature of the motivation behind the behaviour may not be clear, or well understood, but we can be sure that there is one that is driving the behaviour that we are seeing in front of us. Generally, there will be a stimulus that triggers the behaviour, again this may not always be obvious, and it is important never to assume what the trigger actually is, instead it is worth taking the time and observing the dog in order to gain an accurate assessment of the behaviour and its causes. The other thing to consider is that behaviour is not only influenced by the 'trigger', but equally it will be heavily influenced by the environment, the quality of the dog's relationships with the other members of the household, the dog's health, and the dog's emotional state at the time. When we consider all these factors it becomes clear that resolving behaviours that are thought to be problematic is not always as simple and straightforward as we might first think.

Housetraining issues

House training issues fall loosely into two different types, dogs which have not been house trained in the first place and dogs which have lost their housetraining. For dogs which have not been house trained in the first place it is often the case that the training part of the process has not been completely reliable, and subsequently the dog has learned that there is no difference between toileting in the home and toileting outside. This is commonly seen as Autumn turns to winter especially with dogs which have entered the home late springtime. The reason is as simple as the practice of leaving back doors open whilst the weather is warmer through the summer months. The owner will engage in training, standing out with the dog and praising the pup when it toilets outside, however, as the weather turns colder and the doors begin to stay closed for longer, the dog's ability to access outside is restricted and an increase in toileting activity in the house follows. This is due to the fact that there has been no differentiation between inside and outside throughout the summer, and the dog has now had its access to the outside reduced. To get over this potential issue, it is important to make sure that dogs are taught to go outside and to differentiate between in and out, by leaving back doors closed whilst the training process is being undertaken.

Essentially, when dog's toilet in the house it is likely due to lack of access to the appropriate area, anxiety or fear, or a history of being reinforced for toileting in that area. For example, if an owner enters a room to find that the dog has had an accident, the owner's reaction can be significant in the likelihood of the dog toileting in that area once again. For example, if the owner has left the dog alone, and when the owner returns the dog is shouted at for having done the toilet, then many dogs will find this more reinforcing than the aspect of being on their own. This behaviour can progress to the point where the dog toilets in anticipation of the owner's arrival, even potentially thinking that in order for the owner to return, they need to toilet. More concerning is the likelihood that the dog becomes anxious of the owner's return and subsequently toilets through concern and worry.

When we talk about reinforcement, we need to remember that dogs can be reinforced by both positive and negative events, the point is that the reinforcement is the aspect which cause the behaviour to repeat, in the scenario above, the owner shouting at the dog is more reinforcing than the owner's absence, therefore associated behaviours are more likely to be repeated.

The best way to avoid this eventuality is to ensure that the dog is greeted as if there were no accidents present, we would like our dogs to greet us in a happy friendly manner, without any fear or anxiety of being told off.

Equally, when it comes to cleaning up the mess after the event, it is important to use appropriate cleaning products, such as those that are specifically designed for the job, or a biological detergent. Clean the area thoroughly and allow it to dry before allowing the dog back in. By doing this we are effectively ignoring the fact that the dog had an accident in the house, and when we couple this with lots of positive reinforcement for toileting outside, eventually the behaviour will change, and the dog becomes housetrained.

The other reason for dogs having accidents is due to a loss of housetraining, meaning that at one point the dog was clean in the house, however, for some reason the dog no longer is. There are a number of possibilities behind this, including moving house, or a significant life event in the family such as a new arrival into the home, either another dog or a baby. Most likely there is the possibility of a medical cause underlying the loss of cleanliness. Should your dog lose housetraining in this way the first port of call should be your vet, as the solution could be a course of antibiotics and not an involved training programme, however, should the vet find no medical cause for the behaviour then simply starting a housetraining routine as you would with a young puppy, can often be enough to remind the dog of the routine and solve the issue. Should the problem persist beyond these measures, then consultation with a behaviourist is recommended.

Destructive behaviours

Destructive behaviours can range from low level ripping up of found items such as paper, slippers, or shoes, to full blown house renovation. When confronted with a dog which is destructive it is important to take the time to assess the motivation underlying the behaviour, if this is not made accurately then any efforts to change the behaviour will be prone to failure. Owners regularly attribute destruction to separation anxiety; however, this is not necessarily the case, and an assessment of separation anxiety should look at the whole dog behaviour rather than an element. In order to work out what may be motivating the destruction, it is necessary to look at what is being destroyed.

The object of a dog's destructive attention can provide some indication as to the motivation that underlies it. For example, if the dog has focused much of the chewing around the doorway that the owner was last seen leaving from, then it is possible that we should consider an assessment of separation anxiety, once we have made that decision, we would need to look at other elements such as the dog's relationship with the owner when the owner is present. However, if the destructiveness was more focused around cupboards and furniture, it is likely that the dog is feeling somewhat bored as these areas suggest more exploratory and investigative destructiveness, equally should the items be things which the dog is normally denied access to then investigatory behaviour is a strong candidate.

Then we have destructiveness which appears to have more intensity behind it, even focused upon itself, these areas might suggest that the dog is quite anxious and in a more agitated state, than that of a more exploratory, investigative nature.

Dogs have significantly more sensory receptors in their mouth than we do, and as a result much of the information they take in, comes through investigating things with their mouths. Once an item is in the dog's mouth, the shape, texture, and taste provide feedback to the brain and feeds into the dog's emotional state. For example, a dog which is particularly agitated may find a soft toy more reassuring than a hard rubber ball.

Wood is often a target of chewing behaviours as it is usually soft and malleable and easy to rip apart, this provides significant feel-good hormones through the act of chewing as well as the pleasure gained from destroying something.

It is important early on in the process to make sure that the dog gets to see a vet for a full physical assessment as there are a number of conditions which may cause a dog to chew, including dental issues as well as ear infections. There would be little point implementing a complicated training programme if all the dog really required was a course of treatment from the vet. Once the vet has given the all clear then there may be a number of solutions to help the dog overcome the need to chew things.

The first step would be to accept that dogs chew things, the need to perform this behaviour is quite natural and as stated previously, the action itself releases lots of feel-good hormones in the dog's brain, subsequently making the dog feel better and calm anxiousness. Therefore, the provision of plenty of suitable chew items allows the dog to practice normal, natural behaviour. In terms of which objects to provide see the section on *chew toys*.

However, should the destructiveness prove to be more intense, or focused on objects which could be harmful to the dog, or problematic to the owner, then seeking a professional opinion would be necessary to assess the dog's motivation for the chewing.

Separation Anxiety, this is the common term for a condition for a dog which struggles to be parted from the rest of the family. It can be very upsetting for both the owner and the dog itself and therefore prompt intervention would be advised. Separation anxiety is often quoted more quickly than it should be, and a proper assessment needs to be made as implementing a training programme when the behaviour is motivated by something else would be a waste of time and effort and unlikely to resolve the issue the dog is faced with. Instead, it is worthwhile looking at the whole picture to see if there are any other indicators.

"When separated from their owners, separation-reactive dogs may become highly agitated and exhibit various activities evidencing heightened distress or panic, such as becoming increasingly active and

worried in appearance, pacing back and forth, looking out windows, and sniffing or scratching at doors." (Lindsay, 2005)

Aspects of the dog's life such as what the dog eats, where it sleeps, more importantly how it sleeps, daily exercise, and relationship with the owner can all build a picture of the dog's general state of wellbeing. All this information should be used to inform how to tackle the dogs' destructive behaviours. For example, if a dog's sleep patterns are not particularly good, and the dog spends much of the day active and following the owner about, then it has little opportunity to rest and process information, all of this adds to a general sense of agitation in the dog and subsequently one of the opportune ways to release this tension is to chew. When the behaviour occurs due to the absence of the whole family, so that the dog is completely alone, building the dog's confidence slowly, whilst the family is in the home is a good place to begin. This simply requires building the length of time that the dog is left alone in tiny increments, starting at the briefest of moments, simply walking in and out of a room for example, next would be to leave for a little longer, and then longer and so on. All of this helps to teach the dog that the owner leaves from time to time and it is perfectly normal. During these sessions, the dog should be encouraged to settle and remain in a settled state. If the dog shows signs of agitation during this point, then defaulting to a shorter period of time will help.

Secondly, it is important to remember that even if the dog learns to settle whilst the owner is in the home, this is quite different to the owner leaving the home completely. This is because we, as people are creatures of habit, and it is the little rituals that we undertake without realising that dogs will often tune into and start the process of becoming agitated to the owners absence, meaning that by the time the owner actually leaves the home, the dog is in a heightened state and once again chewing and destructive behaviours act as a release valve for the dogs stress levels.

Many texts over the years advised multiple changes to the owner's routine in order to counteract the routines that the dog is tuning into. Some of this advice proved unworkable for many owners and subsequently failed to address the problem, often exacerbating the problem instead of helping it. However, much of the advice is good, and the trick is to make sure that any changes to an owner's routine are practical and easy for the owner to put into practice. The first thing to look at are the little triggers that the dog is cuing into, these can be things such as picking up keys, putting on a certain pair of shoes, a certain jacket, the time of day that the owner has a shower could also be a trigger for example. In order to help the dog, understand that these do not always signify that the owner is leaving is to randomly pick up the keys, put on those particular shoes or jacket or change the timing of the shower. Even something as simple as changing the order in which the owner performs the routine can really help to break the associations allowing the owner to put in place a different set of behaviours instead.

Equally something as simple as saying 'goodbye' to the dog can cue them to the fact that you are not returning.

Working with a professional behaviourist, an owner should be able to work out a changed routine which is practical to implement and therefore most likely for success. Add to this the increased use of chew toys and an encouragement to rest more appropriately and the owner will have a chance of getting on top of the destructive behaviour.

As stated previously, these sections are not designed as a 'how to' solve these complex problems, more they are intended as a guide to how complicated and complex some of these issues can be, therefore it is worth repeating once again that should an owner find themselves faced with a dog which is chewing excessively or destroying the home, they should contact a professional behaviourist at the earliest opportunity as well as arranging for a full health check with their vet.

Vocal behaviours

Vocal behaviours can be one of the most frustrating behaviours to have to deal with as they often take hold in the owner's absence, only coming to light when irate neighbours finally come round to complain, at this point the owner is keen to get a quick resolution to the issue, however, vocal behaviours can be difficult to resolve.

One of the issues that vocal behaviours provides is the fact that very often they are self-reinforcing, there is an internal reinforcement that takes place for the dog, equally it is also a common reaction of the owner to attempt to quiet the dog by shouting at them, which, depending on the reasons for the vocalization in the first place can cause the dog to feel like the owner is joining in with the behaviour and it then further repeats itself.

Vocalisations can be loosely categorised in the following way.

- Barking
- Whining
- Growling
- Howling

Barking is the most overt of the listed behaviours, and the most likely to be annoying to neighbours or passersby, barking itself can fall into further subcategories.

- Alert barking (to a stranger for example)
- Alert barking (to notify that they have been left behind)
- Distance creating barks.
- Distance diminishing barks

Alert barking to a stranger is often the one which is most tolerated, as this type of barking occurs whenever the dog feels that there is a stranger or intruder in or around the property. This type of barking tends to be fast, and is short lived, usually only lasting for as long as the perceived threat is around. It is the type of barking that is heard whenever you knock on the door of someone who owns a dog, and many people feel quite comforted by this type of barking as it is a good way to deter people who would otherwise have ill intentions towards the owner or the property.

Alert barking to notify that they have been left alone, this is the type of barking which causes the most distress, as it usually occurs when the owner has left the property and the dog is on their own. This type of barking can vary in intensity and duration; however, it is clear that the dog is in some kind of emotional distress. Often neighbours find this type of vocalization most upsetting as they feel that the dog is in a position of suffering in some way. This can be the case, but equally it could simply be that the dog is vocalizing in order to call the family back.

Once again before attempting to address this behaviour, it is worthwhile contacting a professional behaviourist in order to get an accurate assessment of the motivating factors behind the behaviour, so as to save a great deal of time being wasted on training for the wrong behaviour.

Some possible solutions involve, management, changing the circumstances surrounding the behaviour, such as increasing the amount of time that the dog is left alone incrementally, similar to the way in which we might deal with destructive behaviours. Where the vocalisations occur in the presence of the owner, it may be possible to teach the dog a cut off command, meaning that the dog is taught a word to tell it to stop barking. In order to do this, it would be necessary to teach the dog to bark in the first place, and then teach the dog to stop.

Finally, it may be possible to teach the dog an alternative behaviour, for example, for dogs which alert bark when people pass by the property, it may be possible to teach the dog to offer a different behaviour, when presented by the stimulus of an approaching person.

Whichever solution is decided upon, it is necessary to get the help of a professional in order to ensure that the solution is the correct one for the dog's particular motivator.

Aggression

"An academic definition of aggression would be: With consideration for context and normal species patterns, aggression is behaviour or behaviour patterns that are used to resolve conflicts, due to threat or challenge, that are ultimately solved by contest or deference. What this means, fundamentally, is that aggression is an adaptation that dogs use to aid them in the 'Survival of the fittest' game. It is used as a means to gain control over important resources or to gain personal space. Aggression is one of many social behaviours dogs use to communicate information to other dogs, humans, and any other species with which they come into contact." (Aloff, 2002)

Aggression is a word which is used a lot to describe a wide variety of motivated behaviours, and although they often appear to be caused by the same reasons, more often than not they are complex and intricate sets of behaviours which can be motivated by a huge number of factors. It is important when dealing with a dog that is deemed 'aggressive' to be as accurate as possible in terms of how the behaviour is being described.

Living with a dog which is showing signs of aggression can be very distressing, many owners find the behaviour quite unpredictable and the idea of the dog they were expecting, and the behaviour offered by the dog they are living with, will cause a lot of tension and confusion in the owners and the rest of the household. In this section we will look briefly at the different types of aggression which are widely accepted as being the motivational causes behind the behaviour. This list is not designed as a problem solver as each case of aggression must be assessed by a suitably qualified behaviourist, this is due to the complex nature of the behaviours involved.

To begin with, let us have a look at what aggression really is. At its most basic level it is simply a form of communication, at the most sedate end of the spectrum we can find a whole myriad of subtle behavioural gestures which are designed to let us know that the dog is uncomfortable, if these do not work, then the dog will move up to a more vocal approach through growling. Growls can be quite low and almost inaudible, through to quite overt and clear in their message. If the vocalisations do not have the desired effect, then dogs are left with only one further option, and that is to bite. Though elements of this process may not be considered aggressive, they usually appear at some point in the escalation of aggressive incidents.

Growling - dogs that growl are polite dogs, the act of growling is a clear communication asking the other individual in as nice a way as possible to stop doing whatever it is that they are doing. If the other individual pays attention and backs away, the growling will usually desist, and the aggressive escalation dissipates. It is all too common for owners to get upset when their dog growls at them, even take offence, especially if what they are trying to do is in the dogs' best interests, subsequently the growling dog gets told off and the owner continues in their course of action. For the most part owners will get away with this and feel that they have trained their dog, unfortunately by telling the dog off for growling, they will learn that as a behavioural strategy it does not work. Therefore, when it comes to telling an owner to stop doing something when it concerns something of high value, the dog dispenses with the growling stage and moves straight into biting the owner in an effort to get them to back off.

For example, should a puppy who has stolen a sock, get told off for growling at the owner when the owner attempts to retrieve it, they may well learn that there is no point in preventing the owner from taking the sock, because as far as the puppy is concerned, the sock is clearly more important to the owner than it is to them. However, should the puppy find a high value piece of food, then this is very much worth preventing the owner from taking it from them, having learned that growling does not work, it does not stop the owner from taking the item, the dog learns that the only way to keep the 'prize' is to bite the owner as they attempt to take it off them. Owners often describe these dogs as 'biting for no reason' or 'attacking out of the blue'. When we look at the situation from the dog's point of view, it becomes clear that the dog felt it had good reason to behave the way it did, and it had tried to give reasonable warning of its intention but was simply ignored. Behaviour does not happen in a vacuum.

When our dogs growl at us, it is best to back away, diffuse the situation and think about other ways in which the situation can be resolved, asking questions such as

- Is the behaviour immediately harmful to the dog or others?

- Is there a more suitable solution which creates the same outcome.

- Can the behaviour be prevented in the future with minimal changes (for example if the dog is growling over stolen items, is it possible to prevent the dog's access to such items)

In most cases taking a step back and approaching the situation from a different angle can produce the desired outcome without placing the dog into a defensive position.

Safety and security - these are often the most significant drivers for a number of aggressive behaviours that are seen in the home. Various things can offer the dog safety and security, from the places and areas that they choose to lie down in, to the toys that they are playing with and the individuals they choose to interact with. For the most part, our homes offer dogs plenty of opportunities to achieve sufficient safety and security, that behaviours such as aggression do not need to be used and subsequently are never seen, however, where there is a degree of uncertainty in the intentions of others, dogs can feel insecure in the situation and feel the need to create space and distance.

For example, Dogs will often seek to rest on furniture, there are a number of reasons for this, however the most significant is the fact that furniture offers the dog the most secure and safe resting space in the house. They are raised off the ground, important if you are asleep, they are comfortable, and they are usually protected on a number of sides, if you consider an armchair, it has the two armrests and the back, this affords the dog protection from three sides and therefore all they need to concern themselves with is the front aspect. If the owner approaches the dog in an angry way, the dog may well feel that it has little alternative other than to try and get the owner to back away. As far as the owner is concerned, the situation can be resolved by the dog simply jumping off the furniture, however, the dog may perceive this action as making themselves worse off and be reluctant to do so. Therefore, as the owner reaches to take hold of the dog to remove them from the furniture, the dog has no perceived alternative other than to bite. Creating an environment in which the dog understands where he or she is permitted to rest, and knows that, when they are in that space, they are allowed to remain without being forced to move, helps to reduce the likelihood of the dog perceiving the owner as a potential threat. Equally if the dog learns that by coming off the furniture when asked, it will receive a reinforcer of equal or greater value, then the action of jumping off furniture is more likely to occur. It is also important to ensure that should an owner find themselves in a position whereby the dog is growling at them over furniture, the best solution is to simply acknowledge that the dog is uncomfortable and sit in an alternative seat. For many owners this may feel like they are giving into the dog, however, it is worth considering that it is better to increase the dogs sense of safety and work on alternative behaviours at a later date. The owner is less likely to get bitten, and the dog is more likely to respond to any training that the owner wishes to implement.

Over the years there have been many opinions on whether dogs should be allowed to occupy furniture or not. There is a school of thought that suggests the dog is more likely to be aggressive and controlling of the owner should they be allowed on furniture, however, there is little evidence to suggest that this is the case. It is also true that the majority of owners actively encourage their dogs to share a seat with them, especially when they are home alone watching a scary movie. As a rule, it is up to the owner as to whether or not their dog is allowed on the furniture, however, I always recommend the following.

- Take it slowly, find out if your dog can be trusted on the furniture with you, some dogs feel uncomfortable when they are in this position, and so by making no assumptions and taking time to find out is just sensible.

- Should the dog display behaviours around furniture that make the owner feel uncomfortable, simply teach the dog to lie in its own bed whenever you are in the room as well. Many larger dogs prefer this as often they can get too hot when cooped up on a couch with people.

- Never force the dog onto or off furniture, instead encourage the dog with reinforcement, and if the dog refuses to move, take a step back and come back to the problem at a later date.

- Make sure the dog has suitable alternative resting areas instead of the furniture.

- If the dog is new to the home, avoid allowing the dog to sleep on the bed with the owner until a solid relationship has been established and the dog can be trusted to share the space safely.

Follow those suggestions and most owners will find that they can allow the dog on the furniture if they wish to. It also goes without saying that if it is the owner's preference for the dog to not be on the furniture, then that is fine too, this owner will need to spend much of their time teaching the dog to lie in its own designated sleeping areas.

It is worth understanding that even in homes where dogs are not allowed onto furniture, should the owner leave the home, then many of these dogs will seek out an armchair or the couch to rest and wait for their owner to return, as the furniture affords the dog the safety and security it needs at this point. It is important that the owner does not chastise the dog when they return should they discover the dog has been on the furniture, as it was a behaviour driven by an anxious response, and therefore, an angry owner coming home is more likely to compound these feelings of anxiety.

For some owners it is the case that they do not mind the dog being on the furniture, however, they do not wish it all the time, and possibly even only on a specific item of furniture. It is possible to train the dog to do this, by simply training the dog to a visual cue. The most common form of this is to provide the dog with a specific blanket, that when placed on the furniture, the dog understands they are allowed to jump up, in its absence, the dog understands that it is not allowed. This method takes some time to achieve, but for an owner who wishes this behaviour pattern, then it is time well spent.

Aggression towards people

Aggression towards people can be broken down into two further categories, they are aggression towards strangers, and aggression towards family members. Both are difficult to deal with and can present themselves in ways which are hard to live with.

Aggression towards strangers.

For the purposes of this it is necessary to differentiate between who are strangers and who are not. I would suggest that when it comes to how the dog perceives things, we can loosely suggest that members of the household are part of the dog's family group, and anyone else can be considered as a stranger. I suggest this because even regular visitors are still visitors, and they are not necessarily predictable in their attendance.

We can further break this down into *territorial aggression* and *protective aggression*.

Territorial aggression would be attributed to a dog which is aggressive towards people who approach or attend the family home, whether this is someone who approaches the front gate or front door, to anyone who enters the home and attempts to interact with the family.

Again, these forms of aggression can be as simple as excessive barking as the person approaches, to full blown trying to bite when the person enters the home.

To understand this type of behaviour it is worth trying to understand what potentially motivates it in the first place. In terms of aggressive behaviours around front gates and front doors, it is common to see highly reactive barking, with corresponding body language, behaviour which is designed explicitly to create distance between the dog and the approaching stranger. However, we equally find that should the stranger enter the property, the dog's behaviour changes to one of calm, almost excited greeting. However, this reaction cannot be guaranteed and therefore it must be assumed that the dog will bite the stranger should they actually enter the property.

As mentioned previously, often owners are quite happy for their dogs to bark to some degree when people approach the house, and therefore a certain amount of barking is tolerated, however, it is important that we can trust our dogs not to harm anyone who has a legitimate reason for being there, people such as postmen, workmen, invited guests and so on. There are two approaches that can be taken in dealing with this, the first is simple management, when people are coming to the home, the dog should be kept separate from the front door in the first instance.

For example, if the dog barks aggressively at the front door, call the dog away and shut them away in another room, or behind a baby gate, enough so that the door can be opened safely. If the visitor is coming into the home, then they can be taken into a room where the dog is not, made comfortable and after a short period, the dog can be brought into the room on lead. It is important that the visitor makes no attempt to interact with the dog, instead they should just act normally, allowing the owner to deal with the dog at all times. The dog should be encouraged to act in a calm and controlled manner whilst in the room with the visitor and close monitoring of their behaviour should be undertaken constantly. It is important that they are showing signs of being comfortable, if not, then they should be removed from the situation and allowed to relax away from the visitor. The process can be repeated over at a later date, with the same visitor if they are willing to do so.

With dogs that display this kind of behaviour I would usually suggest to the owner that they make decisions as to who needs to meet the dog and who does not, many visitors to the home do not stay long and therefore their need to interact with the dog may not be as necessary as first thought. However, there are visitors who will stay for a while, and therefore the time should be taken to introduce the visitor carefully, often starting off site on neutral territory, and allowing everyone to enter the home together. The visitor should continue to make little attempt at interacting with the dog, until the dog indicates that they would like to interact in a calm and controlled manner.

It is important that when we are undertaking the retraining around meeting people, that any reinforcement for good behaviour must come from the owner, we are looking for the dog to display calm relaxed behaviours in the presence of the stranger and be reinforced by the owner. If the reinforcer is delivered by the stranger there is a risk that the reinforcer itself is then associated with something that the dog finds intimidating and therefore loses its reinforcing value. As far as the dog is concerned, they should be able to control the interaction with the stranger, meaning that although they should not be able to behave badly with the visitor, when they are calm, they should be allowed to approach if they wish to. They should ever be forced to interact with anyone, and all visitors should respect the fact that the dog needs time and space to get used to them.

Aggression towards strangers when out for a walk can be motivated by slightly different factors. The first and most common is a failure in the quality of the socialisation period, where the young dog has not learned sufficiently well, alternative behaviours in dealing with the approach of unknown persons, and instead has learned to bark and lunge at people in an effort to stop them coming any closer.

"Dogs who do not have extensive exposure to novel stimuli are at much higher risk for development of behaviour problems (anxiety AND aggression) as adults." (Aloff, 2002)

This behaviour is often inadvertently reinforced by the owner, by making the lead shorter and tighter, as well as verbalizing towards the dog in an effort to get them to stop, all of these actions can be reinforcing for the dog and instead of stopping the behaviour, encourages it instead.

For this type of behaviour, it is necessary to pay attention to the intention of the dog. The initial reaction towards the stranger is designed to create distance and space between the dog and the approaching person, therefore, changing direction, moving away, and allowing space and distance to be achieved will help to reduce the levels of reactivity that the dog is experiencing.

Under no circumstances should an owner attempt to introduce the dog to the stranger, as this will only serve to make the dog's reactions worse. By creating distance, an owner allows themselves the opportunity to create a scenario where the dog is far away enough that they are more able to concentrate and take in any learning that the owner wishes to undertake.

Equally, it was widely thought that the best way to help dogs like strangers was to allow the new person to give the dog a reinforcer, often through the owners tossing a treat jar to the stranger and the stranger then throwing a treat to the dog, however, this method was always inconsistent in practice at best and more often than not the dog would eat the treat and then continue with the aggressive barking. Instead, it is much more effective that any reinforcement should be delivered by the owner, as it is the owner who is the trusted party in the equation and also allows the owner the opportunity to deliver the reinforcer, only when appropriate behaviour is achieved.

Dogs have a reactivity threshold, meaning that there is a definitive distance from a threat or stressor, before the dog feels the need to react. These thresholds vary between individual dogs, and it is not for the owner to decide how far away it should be. For some dogs, the mere sight of a stranger can be enough to trigger the behaviour, whereas for other dogs, it may be a much shorter distance, and also how the stranger approaches the dog, whether it is full on, or whether the person is looking at the dog or not. When it comes to treating behaviours such as this, it is important to be cautious and make no assumptions as to how the dog will behave. Keep your distance as far away as possible and over time, reduce the distance as the training takes hold and the behaviour becomes more manageable.

So how do we build a dog's confidence when it comes to meeting new people?

● Firstly, choose appropriate times of the day to walk, walking your dog in busy places, at the busiest points of the day is more likely to subject your dog to bumping into lots of people, this gives the owner little chance to reinforce calm relaxed behaviour, and reduces the likelihood of being able to maintain distance.

● Be vigilant, when walking dogs which have issues with people, it pays to be as vigilant as possible to the surroundings, attempting to spot potential triggers, before they get too close.

● Keeping the dog on the lead at all times, allowing the dog to run free means an owner is less likely to be able to maintain control of the situation and increases the risk of injury to both the dog and the other person. There are legal ramifications to this equally, therefore keeping the dog on lead maintains safety for all involved.

● Make sure there are plenty of handy reinforcers available, these should be anything which is easy to carry, such as high value food items, a favourite ball, even the owners own reactions and interactions with the dog can influence the outcomes.

● Put the phone away, walking a dog with reactivity issues towards new people, requires a high level of attention, the owner needs to be monitoring both the surroundings and the dogs' reactions.

● Keep walks shorter to start with, but they can go on walks more often if appropriate. It is better to have an incident free 10-minute walk twice a day, than a twenty-minute challenging walk.

When the dog is exercising in its safe distance, this is when the majority of the training needs to take place, this is the point when the dog is most likely to be able to focus on the owner and be distracted from the environment around them. Exercises to practice are simple tasks such as loose lead walking, watch me (where the dog looks at the owner when asked), hide (this is a where the dog is taught to walk directly behind the owner when asked, and only moves out when the owner indicates to do so). The aim here is to build a good history of both interaction and reinforcement in the absence of the trigger. The minute a trigger appears, the owner should attempt to continue working with the dog in the same way, for as long as the dog is feeling comfortable. As soon as the dog shows signs of discomfort at the approaching person, the owner should move away, and get the dog to a point where they are once again comfortable. It is worth noting that as soon as the dog enters into a reactive behavioural pattern, it is too late for the owner to attempt training, as the dog is unlikely to be able to pay any attention to the owner's requests, even the highest value reinforcer will be redundant at this point, therefore moving into a space where the dog can relax again is vital to the success of the training.

In both cases with aggression towards strangers, safety is of utmost importance, as an owner can find themselves prosecuted if their dog is found to be dangerously out of control in a public place or makes someone think they may get bitten. This means that an owner must make sure that they have control of the dog at all times in a public place, this also applies to dogs in the home, and even though they are not necessarily a public place (unless the person has a right to be there in line with their duties - a postman for example). It is particularly good practice to ensure that the dog is unable to harm any visitors to the home.

Aggression towards members of the household

Aggression towards household members can be one of the most challenging types of behaviour as there are numerous possibilities as to why the dog is behaving in this manner. Therefore, it is necessary to seek the help of a professional behaviourist in order to make an accurate assessment of the motivation that underlies the behaviour. It is the most distressing for the owner as it often means fundamental changes to the way they live, and how they live with the dog.

Some of the possible causes to dogs becoming aggressive towards their owners include.

Fear and anxiety

Possessive aggression

Safety and security

Physical interaction - grooming, handling etc.

Pain

Fear and anxiety are a large area when it comes to dogs, it underlies many different types of behaviour and has far reaching implications for the dog's health and wellbeing. It is equally difficult to overcome without some significant changes including the possibility of requiring a level of veterinary intervention to help the situation. There is a difference between fear and anxiety, and they can manifest themselves quite differently. Put simply Anxiety is a level of concern and worry about events that are perceived to happen, for example a dog which is left alone for a period of time, may become anxious about the owner's absence, punctuated with concern over external sounds and noises. Fear, on the other hand, tends to manifest itself over events that have happened, for example the unpredictable bangs and crashes of fireworks can produce quite extreme fearful behaviours. The two are often placed together as the solutions are often similar.

When we consider the lives that we expect our dogs to lead, versus their biological and ethological motivations, it is not too hard to understand how fear and anxiety become an everyday part of their lives. Throw into this mix incomplete or insufficient socialisation and it becomes clear how we find ourselves living with worried dogs. With fear and anxiety, it is also the case that it can take hold of a dog's life, despite the best efforts of the owners during the dog's upbringing, and sometimes it does not take a lot for the dog to end up quite fearful.

In my own personal experience, fear and anxiety has been an underlying cause for the vast majority of behavioural issues that I have dealt with, it is true to say that largely these have been related to the kennel environment, and it subsequent consequences, however, it is clear to see in dogs which have been brought up in loving, diligent homes, where the dog has suffered a couple of unfortunate events which have shaped their view of their world and how they then continue to interact with it.

If we consider that fear and anxiety may well be rife through the dog population then some of the behaviours, we see make a lot more sense. It would be fair to say that dogs are not really that well equipped for dealing with the modern world, with all the hustle and bustle, the constant interactions they need to undertake, the noise, smells and general busyness that they are strolled out into on a daily basis, we maybe need to ask ourselves not how dogs develop fear and anxiety, but more, what are the behavioural skills they use to avoid it.

It is at this point that we should also consider the effects that health and fitness have on dog's behaviour. It would be accurate to suggest that any behaviour which develops without a clear pathway, for example, it is not well understood why the dog has started behaving in this way, especially where the behaviour is very sudden in its onset. Then, the first place to go is to the vet. Many behavioural changes can be attributed to a development in the dog's overall health. Pain in particular is known to have a significant effect on behaviours such as aggression, and where sometimes the source of the pain is obvious to the owner, it is also the case that the pain may be coming from an unseen condition, which can only be diagnosed by a vet. Either way, pain must be treated as soon as possible, as it can have long term effects on how the dog behaves and interacts with the family. Where the cause of pain is obvious such as a sore foot, or other injury, avoidance of the area is relatively easy, however, with some conditions understanding where the pain actually is, becomes a little more difficult. Conditions such as arthritis may be suspected, especially if the dog is slightly older, equally some conditions will be more prevalent in certain breeds, the vet will be able to give the dog a thorough examination and recommend an appropriate course of treatment. It may be that there will still be a need to contact a behaviourist as the dog will need help to learn new behaviours to help it navigate the pain without resorting to aggression, and again an owner should be prepared for a degree of management.

It is also the case that some health conditions may not be so straightforward to diagnose, and therefore a period of working out by the vet as they rule out conditions may have to be undertaken, again this is a scenario where contacting a trainer or behaviourist may well be beneficial. Finally, as with medications that we take as people, many of the medications that are prescribed for dogs to help with one condition, may well create changes in behaviour due to the associated side effects of that particular medication. These side effects should be discussed with your vet and monitored very closely, as they can occasionally cause behaviours of concern to establish themselves.

It is not for a trainer or behaviourist to tell you whether your dog is in pain, that is strictly the role of the vet, however, they will generally recommend that the dog has a full health check before any behaviour modification is implemented, as the likelihood of a physical condition driving the behaviour is extremely high.

Again, when we combine the two potentials of fear and anxiety and a health condition, we can start to see that possibly many dogs are behaving the way they do, due to a general anxiety caused both by the environment but equally by the way that they are feeling. For example, a dog with untreated arthritis for example, may feel quite anxious of small children running around, either in the home or when out for a walk, and in an effort to prevent themselves getting hurt, respond in a way that we would perceive as aggressive, however, they are simply attempting to create space between themselves and the thing that could cause them further pain.

Pain may not be as obvious as having a huge overt reaction, often there are very subtle signs that there is something not quite right. Things to look out for are.

- The dog clearly favours a specific area, maybe focuses on that particular area during grooming.

- Excessive licking of the area

- Unusual fur pattern - the fur looks ruffled and out of line of the rest of the body.

- The dog may look at your hand quickly when stroking them in that particular area, a sharp head turn.

- Reluctance to move, walk or run.

- Excessive scratching

- Hair loss in a particular area

- Head shaking - could indicate sore ears for example.

These are all behaviours which may occur at a very subtle level and maybe overlooked if the owner is not aware to look out for them, equally on their own and as one-off behaviours they are likely not a cause for concern, however, repeated observations of the same behaviours and reactions occurring may be enough to consider getting the dog checked by a vet with the specific area a point of focus.

It is often the case that should the dog find itself being handled in such a way that it is made to feel uncomfortable then aggressive behaviours can present themselves. Dogs which have issues with handling have often had little or no physical interaction from a young age, either that or they have had particularly poor physical interactions with people, equally, if the person is unknown to the dog, then their desire to maintain distance and space is motivation enough to cause behaviours such as growling, barking, and even biting.

Dogs have rules of interaction, much as we do. For example, one person's sense of acceptable interaction may be quite different to others. I have quite a large sense of personal space, I do not like physical contact especially from people I do not know and therefore anyone who approaches me too closely, will cause me to tense up and be a little more defensive than if they were to maintain a safe distance from me. I do acknowledge that this is specific to me and not everyone feels the same way, we are each different in what we feel is comfortable or acceptable levels of physical interaction, and that is fine, there is nothing wrong with that. Dogs are very much the same, depending upon their history and their associations to physical contact and interaction, will dictate their responses when presented with the situation.

As a general rule it is a good idea to adopt the 'choice and control' approach. Much as someone would not assume that another person would want a hug on first introduction, the same would apply to a dog. Allow the dog the time and space to approach you, allow them to dictate the interaction. Move obviously, this is different to moving slowly, as some dogs will find slow movements weird, instead be clear in your intentions. First contact should be in areas where the dog is most comfortable at being touched, these areas tend to be where dogs expect to be touched and these are not necessarily the areas that we would automatically touch them. For example, the top of the head is a common place for dogs to be touched, especially upon first contact, this is largely due to the fact that their heads are the parts of their bodies which are nearest our hands, however, from their point of view, a hand reaching out over the top of their head can be quite unnerving. In general, placing your hands anywhere below their eye line, where your intentions are clear, is a much better approach and one more likely to receive a favourable response for the dog.

By applying the traffic light system to the general handling of dogs we may stand a better chance at interacting with them in a way in which they feel much more comfortable.

Green areas are areas where the dog is comfortable being touched, these generally are areas which are obvious, or which have been conditioned over time- this is generally why we get away with petting a dog on the head, as they have learned that the action results in a brief interaction and the whole thing then moves on, however not all dogs feel comfortable with this.

Amber areas tend to be areas where the dog is not touched or handled that often, these can be back of the neck, shoulders, upper legs, and often the top of the head.

Red areas are areas which the dog is rarely if ever handled. These tend to be the pads of the feet, paws, underbelly, and tail. Due to the nature of where these areas are in relation to the rest of the dog, many dogs feel incredibly uncomfortable being handled in these areas.

To help a dog overcome the amber and red areas, it is a good idea to predominantly handle the dog in the green areas, occasionally touching the dog in an amber area and slowly building the dogs confidence at being handled in this area. The more that the dog accepts being handled in the amber area, it slowly turns green, and the red areas slowly become amber and so on.

If raising the dog from a puppy, it is worth spending a lot of time actively involved in gentle handling, massage, and gentle petting in areas so that the pup learns that handling is a pleasurable experience and not one to be feared in any way. Once the pup is comfortable with this it is then worth asking as many people as possible to handle the pup in the same way, so that they get used to the idea that multiple people will handle them, and it is all okay.

If starting this process with any dog, it is a good idea to undertake a degree of muzzle training.

Muzzles

"A muzzle is necessary equipment for the safety of the handler, other people, and other dogs used as 'helpers'. For dogs who have growled or snapped at someone already, muzzles are required equipment for many situations, particularly when training a behaviour you are unsure of how your dog will respond to." (Aloff, 2002)

Most people will associate muzzles with dogs which are aggressive or dangerous, they are equally often associated with certain breeds, however the truth is that ALL dogs should be taught to be comfortable wearing a muzzle, there are a couple of reasons for this, the main one being that we are generally unable to predict the future, and it is not too much of a stretch of the imagination to conceive of the day when the dog is pain and needing to be examined by the vet, and the difference between a successful examination and the vet guessing is the fact that the dog is wearing a muzzle. Other reasons why a dog might wear a muzzle include it constantly picking up items when out in public and consuming them. This is a common problem and unfortunately dogs can pick up all sorts of items that can do them harm. One of the common ones are chicken bones that have been thrown away after someone has enjoyed a takeout. This is something that I see a lot in my local park, the ground is often littered with takeout wrappers and discarded chicken bones, one's first thought is that the people were less than diligent in disposing of their waste, however, if you were to go to the park early in the morning when fewer people are about, you would clearly see the numerous crows and seagulls raiding the bins and leaving their spoils for all to encounter.

One of my dogs does not bother with the leftovers of others, she might have a quick sniff, but quickly walks on, the other works on the basis that as long as it is in his mouth or stomach, then he will worry about the consequences later. He walks everywhere with a muzzle on, partly due to the fact that he is a greyhound with a love of small furry animals, the other is that it is the most effective way to prevent him from consuming items that would do him harm.

Interestingly most people do not show concern when presented with a greyhound in a muzzle, it is expected and normal for most folk, however, if my other dog, a small terrier type was to be wearing one, I would receive a quite different response for the other people walking in the park.

There are a couple of styles of muzzle which principally fall into two types, the first and most commonly seen is known as the basket muzzle. These are predominantly made of plastic, although they can also be found made of metal, and they simply form a cage over the dog's nose and mouth. There is usually space for the dog to open its mouth, allowing it to pant and breathe with an open mouth, important for when the weather is warmer. Dogs are quite able to drink whilst wearing one, and it is also possible (with a little practice) for treats and reinforcers to be passed through, whenever the dog behaves in a way that is deemed appropriate.

The other type is a fabric muzzle, these are much more restrictive, and have been developed largely for use when the dog is at the vet, as they keep the dogs mouth closed completely. They are not for use with general walking, as they do not allow the dog to pant, and it is difficult for the dog to drink whilst wearing them.

Another commonly seen type of muzzle is an anti-bark muzzle, these work on a similar principle as the fabric muzzles and work by preventing the dog from opening its mouth. As a rule, anti-bark muzzles serve no purpose in addressing the cause of the barking and could end up causing more harm and distress than if the dog's barking were tackled in a different way.

Irrespective of why you might choose to place a muzzle on your dog, it is important that the dog is trained to wear it comfortably and safely. Generally, for most purposes only using a basket muzzle would be the one to choose, they are the most versatile and are most user friendly for the dog. Equally once the dog is comfortable wearing one, they can be used for the majority of situations.

The process of training the muzzle is relatively straightforward as we are needing to make positive associations to the dog wearing it. The easiest place to start is by placing a few small treats on the leading edge of the muzzle, making sure that the mouth of the muzzle is open, and the straps are held back out of the way. Simply allow the dog to take the treats and click and reinforce at the same time. Once the dog is comfortable with this stage, begin to place the treats further back, incrementally encouraging the dog to place its face deeper and deeper into the muzzle, ensuring that the straps are still well out of the way. Once the dog is happy to put its face the whole way into the muzzle, ask them to maintain their position for increasing amounts of time, maybe aiming to get to the count of ten. Remember to reinforce each time. Once the dog is holding their face in the muzzle, then slowly introducing the straps into the process, allowing the dog time to get used to the idea of having them attached behind their ears and the back of the head. Begin this by making sure the straps are at the loosest they can be, and progressively tighten as the dog becomes increasingly comfortable.

Finally, you can undertake muzzle training sessions just prior to really nice events such as going for a walk, or eating their dinner, ensuring that the dog then begins to associate wearing the muzzle with really exciting events.

It is very much worth taking the time to train the muzzle and allowing the dog to take the process at their own pace, as once the training is complete, the dog will actively seek to wear a muzzle, and be comfortable whilst wearing it, meaning that they are less likely to cause themselves any damage whilst wearing it. If you take the process too quickly and end up effectively forcing the muzzle on the dog, then you will find the dog will spend a lot of time attempting to remove the muzzle by rubbing it constantly on the ground, against your legs, or hooking their front paws in and trying to pull it off, all of this can cause damage to the dog and yourself.

Aggression and the human response.

How we respond to our dogs' behaviour often has a direct and significant influence on whether the behaviour lessens or increases, this is particularly relevant when we consider aggressive behaviours. It is all too easy to feel that the dog's behaviour is directed at us by way of a number of factors, from the dog being spiteful, insubordinate, stubborn, or simply just being mean. When a dog acts, it is usually quite difficult not to react, and it is the reaction that we have which will often dictate how the dog responds next. In the case of dogs being aggressive, choosing the right reaction is key to helping change the behaviour. This is not an easy thing to do, as many of us will struggle to control an initial reaction, however, taking a moment and counting to ten will really help to think about how best to handle a situation.

Unfortunately, many responses by owners involve escalating the situation, especially when the behaviour has occurred over something such as the dog refusing to respond to what the owner feels is a reasonable request.

It is still the case that there are owners who will tell their dog off when the dog growls at them, we have looked at the consequences of this action in previous sections, however it is worth asking why we might respond to the dog in this way, what is it about a dog growling at us which could cause us to respond aggressively towards it.

To try and answer this, it is worth considering how the majority of people still understand and believe dogs organise their social systems. For years, it has been passed down through the popular press, social media, and other owners, that dogs have to live as part of a pack, even today there are numerous references to the idea of a 'pack'. Within this concept, the idea is that the 'pack' requires a leader, and logically this leader would naturally be the human adults in the home, closely followed by the children, and the dog should occupy a subordinate role at the 'bottom' of the pack. If the dog shows any behaviour which would suggest that it is challenging this model, then they need to be put back in their place.

For years, as trainers, we were taught that dogs require certain rules for living by, the advice was largely based on a dominance reduction programme, where the dog was restricted in its access to various different elements of the household. Recommendations would include.

- Not allowing dogs on furniture

- Not allowing them through doorways first

- Making sure they eat after the owner.

- Ensuring that their food bowl could be removed from them at any point the owner chose.

However, as trainers it was clear that this advice, that these recommendations were not correct. If they were, if it was truly the case that dogs responded favourably to this type of regime, then most owners would find that their dogs would settle very quickly, however, when rehoming dogs for example, with these recommendations in place, it was often the case that aggressive incidents increased, therefore it was clear that something else was at play.

It was discovered that instead of helping the dog settle in, dominance reduction programmes, and variations therein, actually increased fear and anxiety within the dogs that were being placed. Instead of dogs being grateful that their every move was being controlled, they were becoming anxious of attempting to service their own basic needs, those of safety and security and so on.

A different approach was required.

Further to this, the concept of dominance and hierarchy resonates within the dog owning population at large, this idea that if a dog growls at you, then it is attempting to challenge the owner over the resources that are available.

"Interpreting dog behaviour using the dominance concept has caused a lot of suffering. Owners misinterpreting the behaviour of their dogs, fed by the fear that their dog is striving to take control over them, whether or not it has become aggressive, motivated them to use harsh and punishment based training techniques, totally neglecting the emotions and emotional well being of their dog." (Appleby, D, Pluijmakers, J, 2016)

Add to this model the idea of Resource Holding Potential, whereby hierarchy within the 'Pack' is governed by how many of the resources an individual can control,

"In simple terms a sense of being able and motivated to control resources can be expressed as an equation of Resource Holding Potential (RHP) + Value over Cost. This comes down to; do you normally get your own way plus something you want minus any concerns you may have about the ability of an individual that wants the same thing to stop you and cause you harm." (Appleby, D, Pluijmakers, J, 2016)

This subject remains controversial, even within the professional dog circles, however, there is increasing evidence to support the idea that dogs DO NOT work on a social system of linear hierarchical control.

The history of the concept of dominance and hierarchy in dogs stems back to a study that took place of captive wolves, where it appeared that the wolves had organised themselves into a hierarchy where there was a definitive leader, the Alpha, then all other wolves followed where this wolf led. The study was published, and the world took to it as the definitive answer to the way in which wolves governed themselves. It did not take long for the same idea to by apply to the world of domestic dogs, and subsequently all behaviours were squeezed into this framework as a way to explain why they behaved as they did.

A year after the study was published, the lead author posted an update, stating that his initial findings were inaccurate and that the linear model of hierarchy was not true, unfortunately by this time it was too late, the world had latched onto an idea which fitted their own viewpoint of the world perfectly. It stood to reason that this was the way that dogs organised themselves as it mirrored our own way of organising our society, from school all the way through to corporations and governments.

Even though the world appeared to accept this model of hierarchy within dogs, research and studies continued, checking the theory over and over again. Unfortunately, despite numerous studies explaining a different organisational model, the linear hierarchy concept persisted and continues to be prevalent within the dog world today.

"Our assumptions about social relationships in a wolf pack have undergone significant changes over the last few years. Today most zoologists agree that the wolf pack should be regarded as an extended family which consists of a breeding pair and their offspring (Mech, 1999; Packard, 2003). Most of the problems were rooted in the disagreement between field and captive studies on the social structure and hierarchical relationships within wolf packs." (Miklosi, 2016)

The idea of dominance is difficult for people to leave behind, as it runs so closely with our own viewpoint. Therefore, applying to other species just makes sense, however there are a couple of issues with it which need to be addressed, firstly, dominance in its purest form would only apply to members of the individuals own species, therefore it is accepted that one dog can be dominant over another dog, however whether they are being dominant over their owners is one for further debate and discussion. I would suggest that a dog can act in a dominant manner, however, the debate would come as to whether the dogs' intentions were to overthrow the owner and take control of the 'pack'. I would argue that this is never the case, the behaviours which might be associated with being dominant can often be explained in other ways.

In order to do this, it is worthwhile to consider all the factors that we have been looking at in this book so far. The underlying motivations for behaviour are relevant to how the dog behaves in the face of certain stimuli, secondly, we should consider where the concept of dominance is applied by us owners. It is unlikely that dominance is ever mentioned in relation to how the dog plays, or how the dog sleeps. Often little attention is paid to the dog when it is behaving as we want it to, however, the choices that dogs make in the absence of our attention can tell us a great deal as to the overall motivation of the dog in general terms. For example, just because the dog does not choose to jump on the couch and go to sleep, does not mean that their sleeping choices are unimportant. For example, is the dog happy to settle on the designated dog bed, or do they choose to lie elsewhere, do they willingly settle within the same room as the family group, or do they prefer to be away in their own space.

Are they restless, constantly seeking the owner's interaction, or would they rather the owner pays no attention to them whatsoever?

Therefore, if we only ever apply the concept of dominance to behaviours which are perceived to be contrary to our desires, then they will usually be applied when we are asking our dog to do something that it does not want to do, such as climb down off the furniture. Then, the desire to maintain our status as 'leader' of the 'pack' promotes the use of aggressive actions on our part, and the whole situation quickly becomes tense. Equally, the dog may have learned that behaviours which intimidate people will allow it to get what it wants, these behaviours may also be interpreted as dominant, however, the underlying motivation may be one of anxiousness and worry. We can see parallels in people, there are many of us who are able to come over as confident and in control in situations which underneath cause us a great deal of anxiety, however, through experience and reinforcement histories, we have learned that the confident in control response allows us to navigate the situation successfully. It does not mean that when we are confronted with the same situation again, we will feel more confident, just that the set of behaviours that worked before will work again. The problem here is that if the dog has learned behaviours which are perceived as confident, however, the underlying motivation is one of anxiety, then our response is key to whether the dog feels the need to resort to more aggressive behaviours.

Dominance reduction programmes for example will unsettle an anxious or worried dog and cause them to become more concerned with protecting the resources it needs to feel more safe and secure, subsequently for a dog which is displaying confidence over a resource which is connected to safety and security, such as the couch, I would always argue that anxiety plays a significant factor in the dogs underlying motivation. When we look at a situation with this in mind, it changes our response at the most basic level. For example, instead of telling the dog off for growling over the couch, we may decide to show the dog a different way to resolve the situation, such as receiving reinforcement for coming down, and lying in its own bed, or better yet, a more appropriate couch or armchair.

This is often easier said than done, and sometimes it may be the case that we have responded to the dog's behaviour inappropriately, despite our best efforts to try and respond in the way we really wanted to. Although this is not ideal, and the dog will respond accordingly, it is possible to change the response at any point, so as to avoid entering into a situation of escalating tension and aggression. For example, if the dog growls at us and we tell it off, it is possible to then effectively apologise, back off from the situation and approach it from a different point of view.

This may evoke a number of feelings in owners; however, the point is that in any situation we can take a step back and consider the situation from a different angle and attempt to reach a more effective solution.

This then brings us to an interesting question in terms of training, in that some of the behaviours which are recommended to be trained fall within the scope of the dominance reduction programme, for example, asking our dogs to wait at gates and doorways, maybe as an owner we do not wish for our dog to frequent the furniture, and possibly it falls into the daily routine for the dog to be fed after the rest of the family, does this mean that by adopting these processes we are inherently affecting our dogs welfare. The simple answer is No. The human response to dog behaviour boils down to the underlying motivation in the person, how the person believes the dog should behave and why it should behave in that manner. A dog which is trained to wait patiently at doorways has been taught self-control around situations which could potentially cause problems should they barge through into an unknown situation, If the dog is not allowed on furniture because the owner does not wish for dog hairs to get everywhere, then this is also fine, the training of these behaviours is likely to be undertaken in a calm and relaxed, heavily reinforced way, rather than the confrontational aggressive way which we have discussed above.

Food and aggression in dogs

This subject requires looking at in some detail as it is a behaviour that many owners encounter and have to deal with on a daily basis. As with all types of aggression there are subtle levels to its application and how it manifests itself. As we have seen in the human response, many owners are taught that they need to teach their dogs to allow them to remove the food bowl whilst they are eating. This practice may work when we are training young puppies, however, it is not to be recommended when taking on an older dog, especially one which may have come from a rescue centre where the dog's history may be unknown or at best sketchy. As a rule, it is not a practice that I have ever put in place, nor is it one which I recommend to my clients, and there are a number of reasons for this.

1. The domestic dog generally will be fed one or two times a day, food and being fed subsequently becomes a large part of the dog's day.
2. Food is always going to be a valuable resource for the dog, it is required for the maintenance of life, and this is something that dogs instinctively promote for themselves.
3. If we have asked the dog to perform certain behaviours before we put the food bowl down, then as far as they are concerned, they have earned the right to eat the food without interruption.
4. Finally, it is worth considering what does the dog learn when we teach them to allow us to take the food bowl away mid feed. Most likely the dog will learn that we cannot be trusted whenever we are close to the food bowl, and consequently we are more likely to increase protective behaviours around the food bowl, rather than reduce them.

We can break down these points a little bit further and look at them in some detail. Let us begin with the second point. Food is always going to be a valuable resource. For the most part our dogs have predictable feed times, and the amount is usually satisfactory to maintain a sense of fullness and avoid unnecessary hunger, however, there are many dogs where the desire for any food is a huge motivator to their behaviours. This also means that when they have access to food, it is worth keeping hold of and this can often mean that they are reluctant to share with anyone. If we take a step back and consider this from the dog's point of view, it is not an unreasonable position for them to take, and when it comes to their food, then it is totally reasonable that they should want to have it all without any type of interruption from the owner or other dogs. Further to this, the availability of a resource affects its value, meaning if a resource is abundant then it reduces in value as it is easily accessed whenever the individual requires it, that at least is the principle, however does this concept stand up in practice when it comes to food, the answer quite simply is not really, as food occupies a peculiar position in our lives, no matter how much is available it will retain its importance no matter what. It is true that different food items will fluctuate in importance depending on the needs of the individual's body, but food does not reduce in importance just because there is more of it. True an individual may be more inclined to share the bounty, however it is equally true that they might not.

To look at this in different terms, if an individual won a grotesque amount of money through the lottery, they will initially be very generous and happy to share with anyone they feel is deserving of it, however, as the pot begins to run dry, and the amount of money in the bank starts to deplete then their desire to share their good fortune, although not completely gone, will diminish so that they then become much more selective about who they share it with. If it depletes even further, then the protection of this resource increases. It may be to someone looking from the outside that they still have plenty of money, however, the fear of losing access to the money and everything that comes with it increases the likelihood of a much more defensive set of behaviours. We could consider it is the same for our dogs, they may be happy to share food sometimes, but not every time and therefore we might find increasing levels of protective behaviours depending on the situation and the individual attempting to access the resource.

Dogs work on a me first basis and this underpins much of the behaviour that we see.

Which brings us neatly onto the first point made. The way that we feed our dogs can increase or reduce the level of importance that the dog places upon the activity. There are generally two or three ways that dogs will be fed, the first is that the dog is fed at set mealtimes, this may be once, twice, or even three or four times a day, depending upon the individual's age and needs. Any dog owner can tell you that dogs know what time it is and will begin a ritualised set of behaviours which are often only associated with food times. For example, my greyhound is quite happy to ignore me for most of the day, content to curl up on the couch and chase rabbits in his dreams, however, at the points in the day when he thinks I should be feeding him, I notice that he starts watching me. Very gently at first, with a head whenever I move, even if it is to change position in my chair. If this does not get the required response he will move about on his bed, shifting position whilst staring at me, as if to say 'I'm awake now, I think it's time you were doing something' Finally if I have not responded sufficiently, he will get up, come over to where I am, and stand and stare at me, and he will not move until I have fed him. He does this around his food times, sometimes it can be a lot earlier than his established dinner time, sometimes it is around the right time. The point is he has learned this routine, based on his own actions and the reinforcement that comes from being fed. To put simply, if he stares at me long enough, I will feed him. Once he has been fed and been out in the garden, he will come back inside the house, settle down and get on with the important business of ignoring me again.

For him, food is valuable, he has issues with his stomach and subsequently he is often hungry, therefore he will occasionally try and tell me it is dinner time when it clearly is not.

My other dog is much less bothered about food and will wait patiently until food is provided, she will take a few mouthfuls and then wander away from the bowl. It looks to anyone watching as if she has had enough and does not wish to eat anymore, however, should the greyhound spot the fact that she has left her bowl, he will attempt to go over and finish her food. This action on his part evokes a huge reaction from her, where she runs at him and vocalizes, she then goes back to her food bowl and continues to eat, grumbling under her breath at him the whole time. However, when she has finished what she wants, she will allow him to access her food bowl and finish what remains. She has different needs around food than the greyhound, in essence she would quite happily free feed. This is where the food is kept topped up and the dog manages its own intake of food, however, given the situation with the greyhound, free feeding is not an option as he would simply gorge himself until he made himself poorly.

This set of behaviours is specific to the two of them and both of them are quite relaxed when people are near their food bowls, which makes living with her behaviour really quite easy, however, in the past I have lived with dogs which felt very protective of their food bowls, whether the bowl had food in it or not. For these guys, feed times were always engineered so that they were able to eat on their own, without any other people or dogs around and they were allowed to eat their food in peace. By doing this they were able to eat at a pace which suited them, reducing the need to hoover the food up and cause themselves issues that way. Equally as this became the normal way that they were being fed, the obvious anxiety they felt around the food bowl and people, began to diminish, and although it never completely went away, feed times became a much more relaxed affair. At one point, there was a dog being fed on its own in each room, thankfully over time this was able to change, and the dogs found that they were more comfortable with a specific individual so that they were able to eat together, as long as say another individual was not present and so on.

I have no strong opinion on what the right way is to feed dogs, as it is so specific to the individual dog and the environment that it finds itself living in. For example, if a dog is living in a home where there are small children, it is good practice to feed the dog separately to where the children are, as the last thing the dog would want is small fingers reaching in and playing with its food. Equally if there are multiple dogs, each individual will require a way of being fed that suits it best, often there is compromise to be achieved, but the owner should be aware that being fed in close proximity to another dog may cause an individual a great deal of anxiety. Equally, if it is appropriate to free feed the dog, and the dog is capable of managing its own intake of food, then there is nothing wrong with this method, as long as the dog is quite comfortable with people being around the food bowl.

There are problems with both free feeding, and with specific feed times, as well as benefits, the best approach is to 'feed the dog in front of you'. Adapting your routines to suit the dogs needs within the environment that the dog is living in.

It is still widely promoted that dogs should eat after the owner, as a way of enforcing the authority of dominance as we have already discussed, however, in my career I cannot say I have ever met any owner which actually does this, often when you talk to an owner they will state that 'they know they should do it this way', but in reality they feed the dog when it is most convenient for them to do so. There is a lot of advice on dog behaviour and training, which although accurate on paper and research institutions, will never be implemented by owners as it does not slot easily into their lifestyles, the second issue with this piece of advice is that it does not work for most people, for example, I know for a fact that neither of my dogs would watch me having a cigarette and a cup of coffee for my breakfast and consider it a full and substantial meal. Therefore, as far as breakfast is concerned, they would have to wait an exceptionally long time before they ever got to eat.

Feed times, however, do offer an owner an opportunity to engage in some basic training, simply putting in place a routine whereby the dog is asked to sit, wait and then given an instruction to continue to eat, will help the dog learn a number of behaviours,

Sitting on cue

Waiting

Self-control

It allows the owner to place the food down, without the dog rushing to get to it. Once the food bowl has been given to the dog, then the dog is allowed to eat the food at its own pace and in its own time, we have already asked it to perform a number of behaviours and the ability to eat in peace and quiet has been earned.

It goes without saying, the behaviours taught do not have to be the ones listed but using the food as a way of teaching some behaviours is a daily opportunity. It is also possible to use the cue to eat as a whistle, so instead of saying 'it is yours' you blow a whistle, by doing this we are able to make the association of the whistle to food very strong indeed, which further helps when it comes to recall training.

There is a third way of feeding your dog, and that is by getting rid of the food bowl all together. Instead feeding the dog its daily allowance through other means holds a number of benefits,

1. It gives the owner the opportunity to feed in a way which helps stimulate the dogs brain, making it more challenging to access the food helps to stimulate the problem-solving aspect of our dogs' brains.

2. By feeding without a bowl, it helps to slow down the dog in its consumption of the food, allowing the dog to take longer to eat and subsequently helping it to avoid issues associated with wolfing food down.

3. It is possible to feed in such a way so as to engage the dogs searching behaviours, where they have to search out the food.

This can be done in the form of a scatter feed in an appropriate area.

4. There are a number of products which can help to facilitate this way of feeding, with the Kong being one of the most obvious. The Kong allows the dog to take its time with eating, as well as asking the dog to undertake a degree of problem solving. It also increases chewing activity onto a focused object, reducing the likelihood that the dog will engage in chewing activity inappropriately.

Again, this form of feeding has many benefits, however, it is only appropriate if your dog is comfortable with people being around food, or objects which they associate with feeding, as the location of the Kong after the dog has finished with it, may be unknown to the owner and for a dog who feels protective of it, it could become difficult for the owner to safely retrieve it. However, this does not mean that the dog can never be fed in this way, it just means a lot more thought and care needs to be put in place before undertaking this method of feeding, as it would be necessary to be able to call the dog away from the item so that it can be safely retrieved when required.

Whatever method of feeding an owner chooses it remains the case that the most appropriate way is the one which makes the dog feel most secure, and comfortable, as well as being practical in terms of the household needs.

Living with a dog which is protective of its food. If you find yourself in this situation it can be a difficult situation to navigate, as it often feels as though the dog is able to find food everywhere, however, there are things that can be done which help reduce and ease the situation so that everyone can live together without incident.

Management

Management of aggression is always the first place to start, the object of management is to ensure that the situation is safe for both the owner and the dog. No progress will be made if the dog cannot be dealt with in a safe and appropriate way. Management can be quite disruptive for owners as it often requires significant changes to routine and can sometimes require them to live with a dog in a way which is unnatural for them. This is the most difficult aspect as it is always difficult to change routine. This is because routines are often born of behaviours which are the easiest route to the desired outcome.

The safest way to manage a dog with issues around food is to implement a routine which does not require the owner and the dog to come into extended contact around the food. This means setting up a way in which the dog is able to be left alone when the food has been given to them. This might be something as simple as feeding the dog in another room. Once the dog has finished, it can be let out and shut out of the room so that the food bowl can be retrieved safely a little later on. It may also require all food items to be secured whenever the dog is around, this is slightly harder where younger children are concerned, but some simple common sense acts will help to keep all involve as safe as possible, such as making sure the dog is not around whilst the children are eating, making sure there is not food left lying around where the dog is able to guard it, unfortunately items such as bones and stuffed Kong's may not be appropriate and should be kept out of reach.

The idea of implementing a routine such as this where the food is managed carefully, is to help take the pressure off the dog where food is concerned, where they do not feel that they have to defend their food bowl from anyone coming close or attempting to take it from them. Of course, there will be times when the dog manages to get hold of food items which the owner did not intend them to get, these stolen items are best left to the dog initially, as long as they are not harmful to the dog, then it is possible to take a step back and put in place a training protocol to help with this situation in the future.

When it comes to starting a training programme to help with this behaviour always seek the advice of a qualified trainer or behaviourist, this is because you want to make sure that each stage of the programme is put in place safely and with all elements considered, equally you want to make sure that the assessment as to why the dog is behaving in this way is accurate and therefore any training programme will have the maximum effect. The management element of the procedure, helps to maintain a safe environment for the training to begin in.

There are number of programmes which a trainer may recommend training behaviours such as

> Swapping -this is where the dog is taught to swap an item that it has for an item which is of higher value. This is a useful behaviour for dogs which like to steal objects such as socks and the children's toys. Extreme care is needed when using this technique with dogs which have food issues and should be implemented as part of a larger training programme.

> Multi bowl - this is where the dog is fed through the use of several bowls, with the owner placing small amounts in each bowl, beginning with an amount which can be eaten in one mouthful, and increasing the amounts slowly as the dog becomes more reliable with the game. Again, effective for dogs which do not see the bowl itself as the trigger to the aggression.

Often owners never fully get on top of the dog's food aggression, but instead reach a happy compromise between management and being able to swap out inappropriate items.

Whatever path an owner decides to take with this behaviour it is important that they seek the advice and help of a qualified trainer or behaviourist, as they will be able to implement a training programme designed to keep everyone as safe as possible, whilst the training takes effect.

Conclusion.

As stated at the start of this section, it is not designed to be used as a how to solve aggression checklist, simply it has been intended to outline the many different causes that underlie canine aggressive incidents and has been in no way exhaustive as the list of motivating reasons is extensive. I would never recommend that an owner attempts to tackle any kind of aggressive behaviour without getting professional advice, and certainly an owner should never seek the advice from forums or other internet sources. That is not to say that all advice on the internet is bad, far from it, rather an owner requires advice which is highly specific to their dog and their environment and family set up, as the behaviour will always be heavily influenced by these factors. Secondly, as owners we are often too close to the situation to make accurate and informed assessments of what is causing the behaviour, and by bringing in an objective set of eyes can be helpful in understanding the reasons behind the behaviour.

Equally as previously mentioned, should the dog become aggressive with no apparent triggers or cause, the first place to go is to the vet so as potential medical conditions can be ruled out which would otherwise impede any training programme that the owner wishes to implement.

Play behaviours and the use of toys.

Play is one of the most important behaviours that dogs engage in. It helps develop relationships, allows individuals to establish position in relation to others, it releases a whole cocktail of feel-good hormones, it provides opportunities to exercise, but probably most importantly it helps build bonds between individuals, even if they are of different species.

Play can take many different forms and different dogs will play very differently depending upon experience as well as the individual they are playing with. As owners we often think of play as a specific set of behaviours, however, play can take many forms and sometimes it is play that motivates some of the more frustrating behaviours.

Another factor which plays a role in the types of games that dogs play, is the breed type, if the dog is a crossbreed, we would look to the breed which is apparently most prominent in the dogs make up. Given that different breeds have been bred for different activities, it makes sense that the way they choose to play and interact will vary accordingly. For example, border collies are famous for their love of chasing balls and playing fetch. This is because they are incredibly motivated by movement, and it does not take a great deal to get them focused on toys such as a ball. On the other hand, bull breeds very much enjoy tugging and pulling on items, which is why they are often associated with playing games such as tug of war.

In this section we will look at some of the types of play that dogs engage in.

Chase games

Chase games are ones such as fetch. Many dogs, but not all, will actively chase a ball when thrown, however, most will keep hold of it once they have it until they have been taught to bring it back to the thrower in order for the game to continue in a manner that is enjoyable for both parties. There are many ways to teach fetch, the main one being the use of the game of swaps.

To play this game it is important that you have two toys of equal value, if using a ball for example, two tennis balls would work well. Throw the first ball, when the dog chases it, picks it up, you can then show them the second ball, which is then thrown only when the dog brings the first ball back. It can sometimes take a couple of false starts until the dog gets the idea, but once they have the concept you can slowly phase out the second ball. An alternative to the second ball would be to use a food reinforcer which the dog gets for bringing the ball back, as with other training the reinforcer can be given for approximations of the behaviour, instead of waiting for the full behaviour, we might reinforce the dog for picking up the ball, then bringing it back, then handing it over and so on. Of course, there is the other big reinforcer that is available to you and that is your sheer excitement that the dog has fetched the ball in the first place.

The game of fetch is a particularly useful game as it can be used to teach a number of foundation behaviours, such as sit, wait, a recall and even a down. Once the dog associates the ball to playing, the toy then becomes a huge reinforcer that can be also used to teach close heel work, even in some cases loose lead. Balls are a really useful toy for the game of fetch, they bounce reliably and can be thrown very specifically, they are usually made of materials which are safe for the dog and come in a variety of sizes, so it is relatively easy to find one which suits your dog perfectly. In truth anything can be used as a throw toy, as long as you can physically throw it, however, it is generally recommended that you avoid using sticks, even if your dog decides to bring you a stick to throw, they offer up a myriad of unique problems. The main one being the ease at which they break, causing sharp ends and wayward shards which can easily find their way to being stuck in the dog's throat, requiring veterinary treatment to fix. They have been known to skewer into the ground like a javelin and end up piercing the dog as it runs towards it.

If your dog chooses to pick up sticks it is a good idea to encourage the dog to swap it for a more appropriate toy.

Tug of war

The opinion as to whether to play tug of war with your dog or not varies depending upon who you talk to. There are those that see no harm in the game and play it regularly, versus those who think that it should never be entertained, and the dog should not be allowed to play it at all. From my own personal experience, it very much depends upon the dog, there are many dogs which thoroughly enjoy a low-level game of tug of war, and there are those which take it too far. Many dogs do not enjoy the game and are very reluctant to engage with it, however, you often see owners attempting to engage the dog in the game as they feel the dog 'should' play it. I would generally recommend that if your dog shows an inclination to playing tug of war, that you take the lead and teach it. As with everything in life the game of tug of war has rules, the main one being that the dog should release the object it is tugging on when you request it to. This is important in case the dog has found something inappropriate to play the game with, such as an item of your finest clothing. If your dog shows no sign of wanting to play tug of war, then simply do not play the game, focus on games that the dog prefers.

It has been said that when playing tug of war with a dog, that the owner should 'win' the toy every time. Meaning that when the owner wishes the game to end the dog has to relinquish to the owner. I would suggest that this version of the game becomes boring very quickly, and for a dog which enjoys the game of tug of war, they will usually stop playing with the toy and go and find something else to tug on, such as a visitor's leg. Better than that, the dog should be allowed to 'win' the toy randomly throughout the game, this way we are more able to keep the dog's interest in the game, encourage focus on an appropriate object such as the tug toy, as well as reinforce the rules as and when we implement them. It is a good idea that at the end of the game the owner ends up with the toy and reinforces the dog with a different kind of reinforcer so as to mark the end of the game on a positive note.

When teaching the dog to relinquish the toy, it is important that the dog learns there is a reason for doing so, dogs very much work on the principle that if they have something then it is theirs and there is no reason to give it up, unless of course, something better is available. I always make sure that the dog knows that there are tasty treats available for relinquishing the toy when asked to do so. Each time the dog gives up the toy, it is given a treat, the incentive to give up the toy when asked becomes strong and you can then reliably play the game without concern that it will get out of hand.

Having said that it is okay to play the game with your dog as long as there are rules in place, I would still advise that it is not a case that anyone can play the game, I would keep it to only a few individuals who can be trusted to play the game properly. The problem is that often people will enter into a power play with the dog and take the game too far, this then can cause damage to the dogs' teeth, as well as getting the dog so excited that they are less able to control where they are grabbing the toy, and in extreme examples they may even grab the person causing injury.

Squeaky toys

Again, squeaky toys are one of the most popular types of toys, especially with the terrier types. This is due to the fact that they will evoke the response that most terriers get when they grab a mouse or a rat, and the squeak can trigger ragging and ripping behaviours. Therefore, it is important to assess the quality of the toy against the ferocity with which your dog engages with it. Squeaky toys are often made of thinner plastic, this is to allow less pressure to be applied to the toy in order to get it to squeak, unfortunately the thinner the plastic, the quicker it will be ripped apart, and the squeaky toy no longer functions, instead it is lying in pieces of the floor. One of my dogs is able to disembowel a squeaky toy in under a minute. The problem with this is that the pieces can be easily consumed and can get stuck in the digestive system, again requiring veterinary intervention to sort out.

Thankfully, there are hundreds of different types of squeaky toy available on the market and therefore finding one which is appropriate for your dog should not be too hard.

These types of toys are useful in that the squeak itself is as reinforcing as anything else we have in our toolkit, and if used well, can be used to reinforce behaviours that we actually like or wish to encourage to repeat. In some cases, you can remove the squeaker and use it in lieu of a clicker, if your dog does not like the sound of the clicker for example, the squeaker might be a suitable alternative.

Chew toys

"Chewing provides stimulation and exploratory outlets, psychological benefits, metabolic (e.g., it elicits insulin secretion) and digestive effects, and a variety of homeostatic functions." (Lindsay, 2005)

The act of chewing is an important behaviour for all dogs, if ignored then often we find that dogs will chew anyway and this is often inappropriate as they will chew items of the owner, or objects around the house which are not designed to be eaten or chewed by dogs. The act of chewing releases serotonin and other feel-good hormones in the brain of the dog, and subsequently it is a behaviour that is often associated with agitation and anxiety. Allowing dogs to chew enables them to calm down. Our job as owners is to provide them with as many opportunities to chew appropriate items as possible. Dogs have significantly more sensory receptors in their mouth, all of which feed back to the brain and stimulate different emotional responses, this is why you often find that dogs investigate many things with their mouths, depending upon the dog's emotional state, the dog will choose to chew different items. Certain textures for example may prove to be more calming than others. Therefore, having a range of suitable chew toys is necessary to provide the dog enough opportunity to express this very natural behaviour.

These types of toys are one of the most useful toys available, however they need to be used sensibly. It is not the case that all dogs can be trusted to use them as intended and often the toys will break down into pieces which get stuck in the digestive system. When you first give your dog a chew toy of any description you will need to monitor its use, equally consider that the toy is designed to be chewed and so it should not be easy to destroy. Many are made from toughened rubber, and these are quite good, though the dog will still need to be supervised. Dogs will chew most things if they are inclined to, therefore providing a range of different types of chew toys is a good idea, dogs will also chew different things depending upon their mood or emotional state. It is possible then, once you get to know your dog really well, to know what mood the dog is in depending on which toy they are choosing to interact with.

Once again when choosing a suitable chew toy, the idea is to get one which will last a bit and does not become lots of pieces too easily. Toys such as a Kong are ideal, they have been developed specifically for the job of withstanding chewing by a range of different dog types. They are not indestructible, and dogs will still need to learn how to use them properly, however, they are excellent for encouraging dogs to chew appropriately. It is also necessary to ensure that the object provided for the dog to chew is not too hard. If the object is awfully hard, they can damage teeth and cause dental problems, if not immediately, then certainly as the dog gets older.

There are all sorts of items on the market designed or sold specifically for the dog to chew, not all of them are suitable and care should be taken when buying chews, taking time to look into the product before providing it for the dog. For example, rawhide chews have proven extremely popular over the years, however, they become very sticky and can break off in large sizes, these pieces can get stuck in a dog's throat, especially with dogs which are not used to eating them.

Not all dogs instantly understand how to chew the items in front of them and it often takes a degree of trial and error in order to learn how to eat them properly, therefore whenever providing your dog with an object to chew on, they should always be supervised in case they get into trouble and require a little help.

It is worth having a look at the different types of chew toys that are commonly available.

Kong Toys

I am a big fan of Kong; they produce a wide variety of toys which can be used for an equally wide variety of dogs. The products are of good quality and as, yet I have not met a dog which will not interact with a Kong. They are one of the most versatile toys on the market. When filled with food appropriately they will ensure that the dog takes a long time in order to eat their food, they can be used for dogs which are anxious as the chewing behaviour helps to release hormones which help calm the dog down, and they can be used at times when you want the dog to lie calmly. Once again, teaching the dog how to use the Kong properly will pay off in the long run.

The classic Kong shape is one of a ribbed cone, with a small hole at one end and a larger hole at the other. The inside of the Kong can be filled with any combination of food stuffs that are appropriate for the dog, the idea is that the dog has to work to get the food out, and so stuffing the food in as hard as possible is the aim, though we would not want to make this activity too hard too soon and therefore building the difficulty level as you go a long is the way to do it. Many trainers and dog owners have moved over to feeding their dogs solely from Kong's and have dispensed with the food bowl altogether. This is a particularly good way of feeding your dog, as it really focuses the dogs chewing behaviour, helps keep them a bit calmer, releases lots of lovely feel-good hormones and extends the amount of time the dog takes to eat its dinner, reducing the possibility of complications associated with eating too quickly. Although this is a particularly good way of feeding your dog, it does not necessarily suit every individual dog, and it may be the case that your dog requires a specific diet, not suited to the Kong, or that you need to monitor the amount of food, or more likely, where there is more than one dog, the risk of competition between the dogs is too high. However, it is a method of feeding that can be worked towards if it is appropriate for your dogs and your situation.

Bones

Bones have always been an immensely popular way of providing your dog with something to chew. There are many different bones available of the market, however, you need to make sure that the bone is such that as the dog gnaws away at it, the bone does not break down into sharp little shards that can get stuck in the dog's throat, avoid cooked bones as these are more likely to shatter. Relevant bones from the local butcher are good. The main rules apply here also, make sure that your dog knows how to negotiate a bone, and only really give them when you are there to supervise, especially in the early stages of the dog learning how to use them.

But used properly and provided appropriately, bones are a really good option for giving your dog something to chew on.

Other chew toys

As mentioned previously, there are numerous toys on the market which are sold as chew toys, however, many are made of thinner rubber or plastic and they can be destroyed very easily and quickly, this is an issue due to ingestion of the small pieces and the subsequent veterinary intervention that may require.

When choosing a chew toy, look for toys which are made of stronger rubber or plastic and always supervise your dog when they are using them.

Fabric rope toys

These toys are being included here as dogs will often choose to chew these toys, however, that does not mean they are suitable as chew toys as the fabric can cause all sorts of issues inside the dog's digestive system. If your dog does begin to chew a rope toy, simply take it away and put it out of sight until you are wanting to use it specifically.

Enrichment

Enrichment is the process of providing something which improves the quality of the environment, for example in terms of environmental enrichment, if we give a bear in an empty cage, a treat ball, as long as the bear knows how to play with the treat ball, we have enriched the bears environment, making it a much more interesting place to be. It is often thought that because dogs live in environments which are busy, that enrichment does not necessarily need to be provided, and in some ways the dogs we live with are often overly stimulated, however, all too often they live in environments which, although full of the stuff, are not relevant to the dog, and in reality, the environment is relatively boring for the dog. Therefore, providing things that are of interest to the dog specifically can only enrich the environment and the experience for the dog. However, the provision of enrichment can easily become a source of frustration, if we consider the bear in the cage once again, the treat ball is only enriching if the following criteria are met, a) the treats inside are of interest to the bear, b) the bear understands what the treat ball does, and c) the treats are able to exit the ball at a rate which maintains the bear's interest.

All too often enrichment is provided to the dog without suitable instruction, and subsequently gets ignored, worse still is that the object becomes a source of frustration and annoyance. For example if the bear really wanted to get the treats inside the ball, but the treats were packed in so tight that the bear was unable to get them out, then the ball becomes a source of frustration, this is still a form of enrichment, however, it is not the one we are trying to achieve, the same can happen with our dogs, if we have packed the Kong too tightly for example and the dog is unable to retrieve the food from it, then instead of being something the dog looks forward to it can become something negative. This is an important factor in whether a dog will use an item that we have provided for them or not. It is particularly important when it comes to games such as puzzle games.

These games are excellent in that they challenge the dog to work out a series of tasks in order to achieve the reinforcer, these can be as simple as moving blocks of wood to reveal a treat, twisting a bottle around a post, or having to press a button in one corner to release a treat in another. However, they require a degree of training so that the dog understands how they work. Usually, it is necessary to begin as easy as possible and build the difficulty level slowly. That way we are more able to build the dog's confidence in the game. Once the dog is adept at playing these kinds of games then the limits to what you can do with the dog are only your own imagination. Even though many of them are designed to occupy the dog in your absence, there is still a degree of interaction required in order to make them interesting to the dog.

In general terms play is a particularly good thing, however, as with many other behaviour's dogs can take games too far, for example they can get far too stimulated by the game and the play gets harder and more intense, this is often seen in bull breeds when playing roughly or with tug toys, equally they can become far too focused on certain toys. Dogs which enjoy chasing balls for example can become far too focused, to the exclusion of everything else going on around them. Although we might encourage focus on a ball to help teach them certain behaviours, some dogs can take it too far and this causes all sorts of issues both with awareness of events around them as well as the ability to switch off whenever the stimulus (the ball) is around, subsequently causing the dog to be in a state of high arousal for too long.

Play with other dogs.

It is often thought that dogs will know how to play with each other without any guidance or intervention, however this is not necessarily true, and it is a case that dogs must learn how to play with each other appropriately. For many years, when undertaking their first forays into meeting other dogs, many puppies found themselves in disorganised socialisation 'parties'. This where several puppies would be allowed to mingle, mix, and generally interact with little intervention from the owners. At the time it was felt that these parties were helpful in allowing the puppies to mix with others of their own age group. However, the issue is that puppies are not particularly good at teaching themselves how to behave and interact with others, consequently, many of these puppies grew up to have quite poor social skills, as they had learned to bully others to get what they wanted. As these dogs develop, they often do not learn the subtleties of interaction, and end up scaring other dogs with the way that they play. This in turn can end up with two dogs getting into a fight as one dog ends up feeling threatened and feeling the need to defend itself, all because one of them did not learn to read the signals from other dogs appropriately. It is better to introduce puppies to each other in calmer situations, where there are maybe only a few that can interact together. The owners are also equally involved, watching, and looking for individuals which are feeling uncomfortable so that they can then intervene and change the way the pups are interacting, or even go so far as to remove a puppy which is not having as much fun. These sessions should be reasonably short in duration and always end on a positive note, so that the puppies leave the interaction with a good feeling about other dogs.

Equally puppies should be introduced to dogs of all ages, preferably with known characters so that the pups have good experiences, interactions should be monitored in order to ensure that both dogs have a favourable experience, it is also true to say that not all adult dogs enjoy spending time with puppies, so communicating with other dog owners about their dogs is important. Many puppy classes incorporate a socialisation element with other dogs, however, often these are limited to the other puppies in the class and so the ability to gain access to older dogs is often down to family members, friends, neighbours, and willing dog owners down the park.

Every now and then your pup (and adult dog) will have a bad experience at the hands of another dog, this is not something to be too concerned about, as long as both dogs leave the encounter uninjured. The secret is to ensure that your dog meets 'nice dog' and has a good experience as soon as possible after the encounter. It is also important that as owners we make no assumption as to how our dogs are likely to react, instead we need to observe the behaviour the dogs give us and respond accordingly. By allowing the negative incident to take hold with the dog, we run the risk that our pup will develop a dislike of other dogs, for fear that they will be subjected to another bad experience. By ensuring more good encounters than bad, the dog should learn that other dogs are enjoyable to be around.

The importance of not doing anything.

Modern dog ownership has a myriad of challenges which are specific to our current way of life, the ideal image of ownership in which we take our dogs for long walks where they are able to run free off lead for miles and miles is increasingly unrealistic. This is largely due to the increased number of people owning dogs as well as these owners being focused in increasingly populated areas. The minute the dog steps out of the door it is confronted by a cacophony of sensory cues, from people walking past to the amount of traffic that it has to deal with, add into this other dog as well as random noises such as construction work etc. and we can begin to understand how much the dog is required to process on a daily basis. Certainly, much of this background stimuli will end up being filtered out as unimportant, much as we do, however, there is a period where the dog is alert to the majority of it, especially when they have arrived at a new home or when they are in their developmental stages as a puppy.

As we have discussed in other parts of this book, dogs will deal with potential or perceived threats through the use of fight, flight, freeze responses, these can be very brief, or they can be somewhat protracted and noticeable. The fight, flight, freeze response generates adrenaline in the body, this hormone is designed to make the body much more responsive should it need to run, or fight. When confronted by numerous stimuli which generate a fight or flight response maintains adrenaline levels in the body and subsequently increases the reactivity levels of the dog.

Equally we can maintain these levels where we are in a situation of continually 'doing' things with the dog, whether that is engaging in exercise, play, training or constantly moving the dog for being' in the way'. When we lead busy lives, it is possible that we are continually 'priming' our dogs to react to the next thing to happen, ultimately causing a situation where the dog is looking for the next thing and predicting it, whether it comes along or not.

As much as we should be exercising our dogs, playing with them, and introducing them to the world, it is equally, if not, more important to ensure that our dogs receive generous amounts of down time. This can be as simple as lying quietly on their bed. We are also looking for them to achieve suitable sleep patterns. A dog will sleep polyphasically, this means that they should be sleeping on and off throughout any 24-hour period. They should be sleeping in shorter cycles of up to 1 ½ hours at a time. It may be that they then move, get up, turn around, stretch, go out for a pee, or take a drink, before lying down again and repeating the cycle all over again.

During their sleeping cycles, witnessing REM sleep patterns is a particularly good thing, REM sleep patterns can be easily identified by the seemingly random twitching where they appear to be chasing rabbits in their sleep. This is a necessary part of the sleep cycle as it helps them to cement the information that they have gathered through any given day. Not every sleep cycle will produce REM sleep, but if it is witnessed at least once or twice a day this is a positive thing in working out how our dog is doing.

By contrast as a species, we will sleep monophasically, this is a block of time, often between 5 and 8 hours a night. Whilst we are asleep, our dogs are maintaining their polyphasic sleep pattern, and it is highly unlikely that they are sleeping the whole way through.

It is not uncommon for owners to report that their dog is sleeping through the night, when asked whether the dog sleeps through the day, they will often report that it does not, with these dogs it is likely that we will see other issues building through the day also, behaviours such as higher reactivity levels when out a walk, destructive tendencies, and even on occasion aggressive behaviours. Sleep is important in the ability for the dog to process the world around them and lack of sleep can have a similar effect on dogs as it does on us, making them much more irritable and reactive.

Dogs will also adopt a range of sleeping postures and therefore their beds and sleeping areas should be large enough for them to express the full range. They will often begin curled up in a foetal position, however, as they progress through the sleep cycle they will also stretch right out, sometimes lying on their backs upside down. It is usually while they are stretched out that we will most commonly witness REM sleep. If the dog's sleeping area is restrictive and prevents the full range of sleep postures to be achieved, they are unlikely to achieve a fulfilling sleep and subsequently we might see correlating behaviours develop.

This means also that we need to be mindful of the size of the crate, or indoor kennel that is provided. The crate should be large enough for the dog to be able to stand up, turn around and lie down in, this includes a sleeping stretch. Though dogs are unlikely to be left alone in a crate for long periods of time, it should still be big enough for the dog to be able to achieve REM sleep.

Many people are still reluctant to use indoor kennels as part of their dogs training and general living conditions. There is no right or wrong answer to this, other than to look at the pros and cons of this piece of equipment.

The Crate or indoor kennel must be trained appropriately, it is detrimental to the dog to simply shove the dog in and hope for the best, this is likely to cause the dog to associate negatively to it and subsequently be reluctant to use it, consequently we would expect to see a number of distressed behaviours occur, behaviours such as vocalisations, chewing of the crate and general destructiveness, as well as a severe reluctance to go into in the first place.

If trained correctly the indoor kennel can be an especially useful piece of kit. When appropriately trained the crate becomes the dog's safe place, the area that it can go to escape the environment or situations which it otherwise finds intimidating, this could be something as simple as loud noises happening outside, or as intimidating as a distant cousin's wayward toddler. If the crate is a place of safety and security for the dog, then it offers the dog a place to hide, until it feels more comfortable engaging with the situation.

Another benefit of the crate is that it can be portable, meaning that should you go away on holiday, the crate can come with you and the dog's safe place subsequently comes too. This helps to reduce anxiety of travel and environmental change significantly.

It is important to take time to train the crate, we want the dog to feel safe and secure when it is inside. This means that the dogs should only ever be encouraged in, never shoved in, locked in, or forced in, equally if the dog is settled inside, it can be invited out, but again never forced. The crate should not be used as a punishment (nor should any sleeping or bed area).

Once inside the crate, reinforce the dog with a relevant reinforcer, often simple praise works well, though food reinforcers can be used dropped in. Also, feeding the dog in the crate and making it a really comfortable space goes a long way to making it a nice place to be.

Finally, positioning of the crate is quite important, ensuring that it is out of the way of main traffic, possibly behind a piece of furniture, or even between two pieces of furniture, covered with a blanket so that it becomes a dark space all adds to the sense of safety and security that the dog will feel.

As a rule, the crate door should be left open so that the dog has free choice of movement in and out. Having said this it is useful that the dog feels secure when the door is closed. To do this build the duration that the door is closed, from a couple of seconds to a couple of hours, ideally whilst you are present in the room so that the dog does not feel left alone. Then once the dog is comfortable, begin to exit the room in stages, starting with a couple of minutes and building slowly so that the dog learns that your movements in and out of the room are perfectly normal and nothing to be concerned about.

Many owners will use a crate for the dog to sleep in overnight. This is fine; however, it is worth considering that we sleep monophasically, and the dog polyphasically. This is important as the dog will wake several times through the night potentially, when it does, they will often check the environment to make sure that their companions are close by, once satisfied that everything is in order, they will then turn and settle back down. If the dog is in the crate in a room away from where the owner sleeps, this can cause issues in the first instance, therefore I have always recommended that the crate is initially set up in the owner's bedroom, and as the dog becomes comfortable with the environment and the routine, the crate can be then slowly moved away into a more suitable part of the house. Often owners are against this as they do not want the dog sleeping in the bedroom, however, I would suggest that this approach is temporary and as the dog settles in, its ability to understand sleeping in another part of the house is much less stressful.

When crates are used overnight, with little prior consideration to the above it is possible to find that dogs become quite reluctant to go into the crate at bedtime, further they may experience anxiety behaviours such as whining, barking or destructiveness.

Of course, the use of crates is a very personal choice however, the principles that underlie their use are especially important and should be applied to all sleeping and resting spaces.

To conclude, sleep and rest are often overlooked, or their importance is reduced when compared to elements such as diet, training, and exercise. I would argue that the dog's ability to achieve suitable levels of rest and sleep are just as important if not slightly more important than the other elements. Having said this, a dog which has the right balance of all the elements should be the perfect dog, right?

The problem with the above question is that each dog requires different levels of each element and therefore it is impossible to state that there is one size fits all approach to living with a dog at any stage of its life.

For example, a puppy's exercise needs vary considerably to a young dog with loads of energy, then compared again to an older dog the need varies once again. It is important therefore to assess your own dog's needs based upon your situation, the dog's individual needs and the presence of behaviours which indicate stress, anxiety, or something else which may be indicative of the dog struggling to cope with the situation.

Case studies

This section is called 'case studies', however, it might well be more accurately labelled 'dogs that have influenced me over the years'. The following is not necessarily a list of successes and achievements in the world of dog training, rather, those dogs whose behaviours challenged me at the time, where there were often sleepless nights and much head scratching. Each one however, taught me something about how dogs learn and how they sometimes struggle to fit in with our lives in the way that we want them to.

Tag

Tag was a two-year-old brindle lurcher which we adopted from a well-known rescue centre. He was incredibly people friendly, and in kennels was very over the top in all of his behaviours, greeting enthusiastically usually with his mouth, grabbing hold of your clothes, and dragging you around. This behaviour had put many people off him, however, it was not a behaviour that we felt was too much of a problem. He had come into the rescue centre with little in the way of a history and therefore not much was known about him prior to being in the rescue.

It was not long after adoption that we discovered that he had quite severe destructive tendencies, and he would chew anything that he was able to reach. Items included socks, clothes, personal items, as much as shoes, doors and even on one occasion, brick. The initial thinking was that it was likely that he was struggling with being left alone for any length of time, and therefore he began coming to work where he was able to spend time with people and was rarely alone, however, there would be times when he would need to be left and so we needed a plan to help him learn to cope being left alone. At this point in life, we were lucky in that we were in the process of renovating our home and as such there were plenty of rooms where if he were left, he would not be able to create too much damage, and, more importantly there was nothing which would be able to damage him.

Once the room had been set up, we implemented a system of leaving him alone, starting out for very short periods, building slowly to longer and longer periods of time, eventually he would be able to spend up to a couple of hours in that room without causing any damage, however, it became apparent that we had started to create an unsustainable situation, in that largely the training would happen whilst we were still in the home, with occasional trips out without him, and this did not sit well with why we adopted him in the first place, as he was to be part of the family and therefore spend time with us, needless to say this training slipped as we became complacent and routine set in.

One other aspect of Tag was that he was not overly fond of other dogs. It was not the case that he completely hated other dogs, and in kennels had a couple of other doggy friends, however we did know that he was specific about the dogs that he accepted into his personal space. Once he was home this quickly manifested itself in quite energetic reactivity should he see other dogs when he was out for a walk. Again, this did not necessarily phase us as it was a behaviour that we had been expecting, though we had not counted on the intensity of the behaviour. Once again, a systematic approach to keeping him calm around other dogs was adopted, this included teaching him to walk better on the lead, as well as walking at times and in places where the likelihood of bumping into other dogs was significantly reduced.

Despite the problematic behaviours we were encountering, he proved to be a lovely dog to live with, especially whenever you were sitting quietly in the evenings with him where he would sit on the couch with you and be quite happy to cuddle in.

It was not long after adopting him that we had started to notice a degree of hair loss along both his flanks, realising that this was not normal it was arranged for him to see the vet.

A couple of blood tests later confirmed that he was suffering from hypothyroidism, a condition commonly found in dogs which can cause a number of behavioural consequences including hyperactivity and aggression. This diagnosis went some way to explaining the behaviours that we were seeing in him, though the destructive chewing remained an issue and though treatment for his thyroid might have an effect on the chewing it was unlikely. It was discussing this point with the vet which caused the vet to check his ears. He had already been given a clean bill of health by the rescue centre's vet, and an initial look in his ears showed that his ears were a little dirty, but of no real concern. Ear drops, and thyroid medication in hand we returned to our routine and waited for the medications to take effect. The thyroid medication had a significant effect, his hair began to return, and the intensity of his reactivity lessened, the behaviour did not disappear completely, and it was not expected to, however, it lessened enough to allow the training that we were putting in to have a more profound effect.

However, the ear drops were having no effect at all, and after a couple of weeks he was back at the vet for a further checkup. This time the vet dug a little deeper and discovered that there was in fact quite a chronic infection deep in his inner ear, which had been clearly causing him a good deal of discomfort for some time. The solution was an aural ablation, this is where another hole is created in line with the ear canal, preventing dirt and debris building up and allowing the ear to clear itself appropriately.

Once he had recovered from this operation, the destructive tendencies all but disappeared. He would of course chew items from time to time, but these would be things that we had left lying about inadvertently and things that any dog would chew given half the chance. The difference in him was quite significant.

Life with Tag was not boring, and he was one of the dogs which taught me a great deal about how behaviours are not always what they first appear. Much of Tag's issue with life was born from the pain and discomfort that he had felt from the infection in his ear, as well as the obvious effects of hypothyroidism. Once these two things had been brought under suitable control, his ability to learn and cope with life significantly improved, and although he remained reactive to dogs for the rest of his life, his tolerance of them increased, and the distance before he reacted reduced significantly. By the time he passed away, he was living with a young child and two other dogs in relative harmony.

Tawney

Tawney has already been mentioned before so it felt appropriate to expand on his behaviour a little more as he turned out to be one of the more interesting characters that we took on.

Tawney came into the home following Tag, and due to Tags issues around other dogs it took a little while for him to become fully integrated. Therefore, he stayed in kennels a little longer than usual whilst the introductions to Tag were undertaken. He had come to the kennels as a stray and therefore we had no knowledge of his history or the life he had before. He was estimated to be about 18 months old when he arrived, but he could have been a little younger. Whilst in kennels he was one of the friendliest, happiest dogs that lived there, and it was felt that his personality would compliment Tag well. The introductions eventually over, Tawney moved in. At this time Tag was allowed to sleep in the bedroom, he had his own chair in the corner, but would invariably end up on the bed through the night, happily shoving us off the bed as he stretched himself out. It followed, therefore, that Tawney too, would be given access to the bedroom, and a bed area was set up for him. The first few nights went without incident, and it appeared that all would be well with this system. The two dogs, even though they now got along, did not enjoy each other in their space and therefore they both had their own sleeping areas.

Tawney would often choose the bed on the floor while Tag would end up on the chair. The first sign of an issue was when Tag would move through the night, we would be woken up by Tawney shouting at him, only to find that Tag would be standing with tawney baring all his teeth at him due to the fact that Tag had moved too close to Tawney's bed. It is worth pointing out that both dogs had access to other equally comfortable sleeping areas which were not in the bedroom, and they could easily have gone and slept elsewhere, however, they both chose to be in the bedroom with us.

Considering that he had only been in the home a couple of weeks, it was felt that the best way forward was to monitor his behaviour and correct the environment enough to allow the two dogs enough space to move around in the night without going too close to each other. This mainly ended up being Tag on the bed with us from the minute we went to bed, and through the night this system seemed to work out okay.

Over the next few weeks Tawney's behaviour around his bed area increased in intensity towards not only Tag, but also towards us. The main issue was that he would give away little in terms of his intention, until he was in full launch, shouting at us for getting too close.

The fact that Tawney felt that his sleeping area needed defending was in itself not an issue, and in many ways was a reasonable response to the change in environment and social situation. The situation was suitably managed by ensuring that he had plenty of spaces where he would be able to rest and sleep without risk of being disturbed. It was the fact that there was little warning prior to his reactivity, there was usually no growling, little noticeable change in his body language, simply he would go from lying quietly to fully standing with teeth bared.

As previously mentioned, there was another element to Tawney's behaviour in the way that he would conduct himself when interacting with people. For the most part, a large proportion of his time with us, Tawney was a friendly, happy dog, who enjoyed meeting new people and was always happy to see you when you came home having been out. He occasionally chewed things, had occasional house-training issues, (mainly if he were poorly), and generally could be considered a normal dog. However, his behaviour when being interacted with physically was of concern.

It quickly became clear that as owners, we needed to become more aware of the subtleties of his body language than we had been with Tag. Once we had understood that it was important for Tawney to have control over his own interactions, allowing him to walk away from contact when he wanted to, allowed us to build confidence in him when being petted. This meant that we could work slowly, building up his confidence at being handled for longer and longer amounts of time. Using non-contact as a reinforcer, as much as we used food treats or even games, (he was quite playful at times).

Over the years it was the case that even though he was never completely at ease with being handled everywhere, it reached a point where we were able to handle him in ways that were necessary, Veterinary treatment etc., however, certain handling would continue to be challenging, areas such as underneath his body, remained somewhere which we could only touch if he was muzzled, thankfully, the need to handle him in this area never arose.

The lesson that Tawney taught us was that often dogs communicate with us on very subtle levels and that as owners we need to be aware that our interpretation of behaviours is often inaccurate and that we should be open to the fact that dogs do not necessarily always want our attentions and will often simply tolerate our affection.

Application of this approach towards Tag, improved the quality of our interactions also, where he was enabled to dictate the timings and durations of our interactions to suit his needs.

Dog A

Throughout my career I have had the privilege of working with numerous dogs, and some have stood out more than others, dogs that I have named in these case studies, are those that have lived with me in my home, however, there have been many dogs which I have worked with which have changed my understanding of how behaviour affects the dog-human relationship. Dog A was one such dog.

Initially he arrived in kennels having been a stray and had been placed for rehoming after having undergone his intake assessment. There were no behaviours seen which flagged as problematic and as such he did not present anything other than a standard rehoming proposition. However, he remained in kennels for a number of weeks, which in turn became a couple of months and due to this we witnessed a deterioration in his overall behaviour. He was always able to be kenneled with another dog, however, his frustration on lead around the centre was increasing, and he had begun to redirect towards his handlers when his frustration levels became too much.

Because of this he underwent a specific training programme and the type of home that was required for him became a bit more specialised, this meant that the likelihood of his finding a suitable home quickly became much less likely.

The behaviours that Dog A was exhibiting were not in any way unusual and were part of everyday life for many kennel dogs, as the environment itself was particularly challenging for a lot of the dogs that stayed there. However, he managed to form strong bonds with his handlers, and maintained a suitable quality of life.

Due to the fact that he had spent so much time in kennels, surrounded by a familiar environment, being handled by familiar people, it was not until he eventually managed to find a home, that a particular behaviour was not picked up. This behaviour was one of reactivity and aggression towards new people. Both visitors to the home as well as people on the street or in the park, Dog A would react violently towards the person, lunging and barking, something which proved understandably problematic for the home, and he was consequently returned to the centre, with a poor history, essentially preventing him from being rehomed again without significant intervention.

The problem faced by the staff at the centre was that he presented little issue to his handlers and to the people he met on a day-to-day basis, as each of the handlers was well known to him, and relationships established and fixed.

There was no issue with his general training, he was very responsive and learned quickly, he soon became quite easy to walk, responsive to his handlers and was taught a number of behaviours designed to counteract his issues with people approaching. Behaviours such as hiding behind the handler, looking to the handler for guidance, and so on. These behaviours however, remained as simple management tools and subsequently his ability to be rehomed was difficult. Any new home would need to spend a long time to get to know him before they took him home, and this kind of home was rare.

The story of Dog A is one which does not end as we had hoped, it was always felt that the right home would arrive, but it never did, eventually the strain of kennels and a couple of handler changes had the effect of breaking his training down and he ultimately began to cope less and less in the environment, with the consequence of his behaviour deteriorating equally. He was eventually euthanized due to a rather unfortunate bite incident.

The reason that the story of Dog A is significant is in the way that his coping mechanisms were stable when his environment was predictable and secure, even though this was in itself a kennel environment. The relationships he had formed with his handlers allowed him to navigate the days without incident, it was only when these secure elements were changed that he found it difficult to fall back on his training. Now, it could be that the training was not strong enough in every available situation, however, it is my belief that the training ultimately produced a false positive. His general responsiveness to his handlers and to the environment that he found predictable and secure meant that the underlying cause of his aggressive responses was never sufficiently addressed.

The point being that when we are dealing with problematic behaviours training alone is not sufficient in terms of remedying the problem, it is always necessary to address the underlying motivation in some way, otherwise one runs the risk of the behaviour coming back stronger and more intensely than it had been before.

In the case of Dog A, given his situation, the fact that he had come in as a stray and the nature of the kennel environment, it could be argued that the underlying cause of his behaviour would never have been sufficiently addressed and that the kindest thing would have been to euthanize him earlier, however, given that he had a quality of life in kennels for the most part, it was worth working with him, in case the right home came along, which could have given him the opportunity to find the safety and security he required in order to settle properly.

Dog A has stayed with me as he was a significant point in my training career, he showed that teaching a set of behaviours to counter a problematic behaviour, will go only so far in helping a dog negotiate life, and that these learned behaviours can break down, when presented with a significant change in their lives. This meant that the approach to the rehabilitation of subsequent dogs would be different, with a greater emphasis on treating the underlying cause rather than training 'over the top' of the behaviour.

Spencer

It is worth at this point to introduce Spencer. I first met Spencer when I started working in kennels, and at that point he had already been resident there for at least six months. He is of interest as he had an almost identical history to Dog A, and upon his one unsuccessful rehoming at this point had demonstrated that he too had issues meeting new people and had returned to kennels having bitten a couple of people (though it is worth noting that the bites were not bad bites and had not broken the skin). Spencer was a medium sized crossbreed and was approximately 18 months old when I first met him. From the outset Spencer proved to be an exceptional dog, despite his issues with people, once he had learned to trust someone, then he would allow pretty much any type of handling and interaction to take place. However, his strength lay in his ability to communicate, both with other dogs as well as with people, once the pieces of body language were understood well enough. Spencer quickly became a particularly useful dog whilst in kennels as he was really particularly good at helping other more 'agitated' dogs, he would be able to help calm them down and would be able to indicate what the other dog was really motivated by. He was known as a 'stooge' dog. This is a dog which a trainer knows so well that they are able to read their body language and use that to interpret the subtlety of interactions with less well-known dogs. Stooge dogs are able to aid a trainer in assessing newer less well-known dogs and subsequently devising a relevant and suitable rehabilitation programme. Spencer was excellent in this role and during his time in kennels, helped numerous dogs cope with the stresses and strains of kennel life.

He was eventually rehomed and managed to live successfully with his new family, until their circumstances changed in such a way so as to adversely affect Spencer's welfare. It was at this point that he came to live with us.

Spencer settled into the home relatively quickly, this was helped by the fact that we had a well-established relationship already, and he already knew a couple of the dogs in the home. He was allowed to settle as he wished, plenty of sleeping areas were set up, and he was never forced to be in his bed or leave it. The dogs were allowed on furniture if they wished, though only Tag ever really chose to get on the couch, the others were content to lie in their own bed areas. As he settled, it became clear that his presence was having an effect on the other dogs, mainly in a positive way. Both Tag and Tawney would on occasion have their usual stand offs, where Tawney would take offence at something Tag had done and feel the need to tell him off, it was at these points that another of Spencer's skills made itself apparent. He would hear the confrontation, often seeing it build, and then quietly and purposefully place himself between the other two.

This action helped to diffuse the tension between Tag and Tawney and the interaction between them would de-escalate a lot quicker than it would have had Spencer not gotten involved. The more interesting knock-on effect of this behaviour was a noticeable relaxation in Tawney. The instances where he reacted, the overall tension in his body seemed to change, and he showed signs of playful behaviours more often and with more people.

Spencer remained with us until he eventually passed through old age, throughout that time he showed no inclination to bite, he was happy to greet people as long as they were not full on with him, and as long as they allowed him to choose the interaction, he would warm to them very quickly. In the end he proved that a combination of environment, time and space enabled him to relax enough so that he was able to feel safe and secure.

It was a year or two after Spencer arrived that we sadly lost Tag, leaving a significant hole in the home. Though Tawney and Spencer got along well, Tawney was not the kind of dog which enjoyed close contact with other dogs, and this was something which Spencer would look for. After much discussion it was decided that we would bring another dog into the home, but this time we would not take on a dog that required rehabilitation, but start from scratch instead, with a puppy. The only caveat was that the puppy must be sourced via a rescue centre.

It was also felt that as there were young children in the home, a puppy would be more beneficial as it would be possible to raise the pup and the children together.

Nala

Nala joined us a few months later. Nala was a Japanese Akita and the only puppy that I have ever raised. She warrants a mention in this section as it is my belief that one of the reasons, she turned out to be such a stunning dog was not necessarily just down to the way that we raised her. She was given a huge head start even before she came to us.

We were lucky in that even though we sourced Nala through a rescue, she and her litter mates had only come into the centre as the owner wanted them to find good homes and she felt that the centre would be able to find them more effectively than they could.

Most significantly, the owner had both parents, and had allowed them both to raise the puppies to the age of 14 weeks before they even considered putting the puppies up for adoption.

This is a rare situation to come across as most puppies are made available to adopt from the age of 8 weeks, often having had no experience or interaction with any other dog than their mother. For the most part this is not a problem, and the new home compensates for a lack of parental input, by attending puppy classes, socialising the puppy, and generally providing good care and attention, however, it is also possible to trace many behavioural issues to this particularly important early stage.

This stage of a puppy's development is a complex time and is influenced by a large variety of factors, and it would not be accurate to suggest that dog behavioural problems all stem from this period in a dog's development, however, should a dog develop a behavioural issue, it is always worth looking at this point in the dog's life. The longer that a puppy can be left with its parents, the more likely it will be to learn useful life behaviours such as how to get along with other dogs, the subtleties of communication, even everyday things such as differentiating the noises of an average household can be handled by the parents more effectively than a loving home. When Puppies come away at eight weeks, the emphasis then falls on the new owners to fill the gap in the puppies' understanding of the world.

Nala turned out to be one of the best dogs that I have lived with, she was incredibly easy going, friendly with people and dogs, though she knew how to make sure dogs behaved appropriately around her. Her bond with Spencer proved to be incredibly strong, and would happily allow him to share her bed, letting him curl up with her. She was respectful of Tawney and allowed him space when he needed it, however, she managed to entice him to play regularly and would play for as long as he wanted without pushing it further. It was Nala's ability to read other dogs which made her so special, throughout her life she was subjected to many different dogs, of all types of temperament, and with each she was able to adjust her interactions to suit the individual she was interacting with. She was a large dog and weighed in at just under 45kg when she was an adult, however, she would play according to the dog (or person) that she was with, playing more roughly with larger dogs which enjoyed that kind of game, and softly and slowly with older or smaller dogs, making sure not to use her weight against them. One example of this was a small terrier which came to stay with us for a short period, she was quite nervous of people, and a little in awe of the world, however, she bonded with Nala quite well and the two of them would play a lot. However, Nala would never stand up during their games, instead she would lie down and play at the level of the terrier. This tactic helped the terrier settle in much quicker than if Nala had not been there, and subsequently she was able to go and live in a family with a number of other dogs, which may not have been possible without the time spent gaining confidence with Nala.

It is not to say that Nala was perfect, and it is true that there were a couple of areas in which we failed her. One of these was in the area of her socialisation, as with any puppy a lot of work went into teaching her about the world and introducing her gently to the sights, sounds and smells of the modern world, however, we fell into the common trap of only really focusing on the elements that were present in our lives at the time. This meant that as she grew older and life changed, she displayed signs of anxiety when new things came along unexpectedly. For example, when we first got her, we lived in a reasonably rural area, and even though we would spend a lot of time getting her used to traffic and streets, this would not necessarily be every day, because put simply it was not our everyday. Subsequently, when life changed and we moved to a more built-up existence, it was clear that we had to undertake a degree of socialisation once again, taking it slowly to introduce her to her new life. This discovery was quite important as it proved that the process of socialisation is an ongoing thing and something which we as owners need to be aware of, that even though the work on socialising the puppy was undertaken effectively and well during the early years, subsequent significant life changes can highlight areas in the dogs understanding which are flawed.

Thankfully, with a good history of socialisation and training, the introduction to new things was fairly straightforward for her, however, the assumption that she would manage without any form of intervention was the key point.

Socialisation chart

Notes to completing the chart.

Each section lists a number of scenarios and situations which puppies often react to. Use the chart to try and tick off as many of the different aspects as you can, trying to meet each of them at least once in the block of eight weeks. Some elements will be achieved regularly, and some will be a struggle to achieve depending upon your circumstances. The point is that you attempt as many as you can and that each of the introductions is as positive and rewarding as possible.

Environments

When introducing to new environments take your time and go at the puppy's pace, encourage happy confident behaviour, and reinforce this. If the pup shows concern or worry, wait, and build its confidence again before continuing on. Some environments will need a lot more work than others, for example asking your puppy to cope with a town centre will take a lot more than introducing it to your friends living room.

Vehicles

Vehicles pose a problem on a few fronts, the first is that they move passed the puppy and any reaction is reinforced by the vehicle moving away, for example if the puppy barks at a car as it passes, and the car moves off, then the puppy learns that barking at cars makes them go away. The second problem is that they sound quite different and so it can take a while for the puppy to generalise that just because one vehicle is no threat then they are all no threat. Finally, it is necessary not to assume that just because your pup will travel in the car, that they actually enjoy it, normally travel in vehicles is one the scariest things for an animal, therefore taking time to build the pups confidence slowly will pay off in the long run.

Sounds

We live in an incredibly noisy world; it is essential therefore that we get our puppies used to as many sounds as we can and teach them that they are largely to be ignored. Some sounds the puppy will hear all the time every day, others are only occasional, for example fireworks. For the less often sounds it is possible to find audio samples of these sounds and play them at low level, building the volume as the puppy becomes more used to them.

People

As puppies grow, they learn to identify things by both their movements and their outlines, this means that the puppy becomes used to the movements and outlines of the individuals it lives with, however, anyone who is different to this becomes a source of worry and concern and the dog can react. The solution is to expose your puppy to as many different types of people as you can find, the whole time ensuring that the experience is as positive and friendly as possible.

Other animals

with other animals some of the exposures will be interactive as would be the case with other dogs, some will be passive, where the dog is just allowed to see and smell them such as with livestock and wildlife. When introducing your puppy to other animals, take it slowly and allow the other animal to control the interaction, not all dogs for example like puppies, and cats always need to feel that they can escape from a situation. Keep the exposure fun and try to avoid allowing the puppy to become over excited.

Environments	Week 1	Week 2	Week 3	Week 4	Week 5	Week 6	Week 7	Week 8
Unknown /new house								
Vets' surgery								
Town centre								
park								
beach								
Country walk								
Café/restaurant								
Carpeted room								
Slippery floor								
Children's play area								

Vehicles

Cars (passing)								
Buses (passing)								
Motorbike								
bicycle								
Lorries								
Cars (journey in)								

Sounds

Baby crying								
Children playing								
Shouting								
Sudden noises (bangs etc.)								
Clapping								
Loud music								
Busy street								
Vacuum cleaner								

hairdryer

Washing machine

Lawn mower

Kitchen equipment

Power tools

Doorbell/door knock

Other – note any sounds that your puppy reacts to

People

Adult men

Adult women

Young children 0-4

Children 4-8

Children 8-12

teenagers

Middle aged

elderly

Wheelchairs/ walking aids

Loud and confident

Shy and quiet

Delivery people

joggers

uniformed

High Viz

Hats

Glasses

Long hair

Short hair

Motorbike helmets

Umbrellas, raincoats

Walking sticks /
canes

Pushchairs/ buggies

Other animals

Adult dogs (male)

Adult dogs (female)

puppies

Cats

Small pets

Birds (flighted)

Ducks/geese/
chickens

Cows/sheep etc.

Wildlife – deer/
rabbits etc.

Horses

Miscellaneous

Progress chart

Week 1

Week 2

Week 3

Week 4

Week 5

Week 6

Week 7

Week 8

Socialisation is a lifelong process; this guide is simply a way to get you started. If you maintain the process of introducing novel situations in a calm and positive way throughout the dog's life, you are enabling the dog to adapt to any changes that may arise in their lives, allowing them to cope.

Training log

Exercise..

Date...................................

Introducing the exercise (write down which method used for beginning the behaviour, captured, lured, and so on, as well as making a diary of progress along with any problems encountered)_____

Exercise   achieved..

Date.................................

The last word

It may be that the career that I have had over the last twenty to thirty years was unintentional originally, however, it has proven a very varied and challenging career, often frustrating but always ultimately rewarding. Dogs, as with all animals, have the ability to bring a great deal of joy and happiness into our lives, however they can be challenging in equal measure. It is also the case that even if an owner does everything correctly, behaviours can still occur which come out of the blue and surprise. There are hundreds of trainers and behaviourists around to help out with any behaviour problems that an owner may be encountering, however each one has an area in which they specialise more. It is not necessarily that every trainer can help with every problem, therefore it is worth taking the time to research the trainers in the local area and find one which specialises in the problem that is needing to be corrected.

So how does someone go about finding a trainer? There are many ways to go about this, but I would always suggest that there are two main sources of finding a suitable trainer, the first would be to check with your local vet, they will usually have a particularly good idea of what trainers are working in the area as well as having an idea of what areas they specialise in. Failing that, another good source is the local dog walking community, asking about on local community internet forums, speaking to other dog walkers in the park (if you are up to it), checking with the local pet shop, are all excellent ways of finding out about the different trainers around. Word of mouth recommendation is one of the best ways a trainer can be promoted as it means that a client has had a good experience and would suggest others go along too.

Finally, there is the internet itself, most trainers will have a website or Facebook presence, and this allows an owner the opportunity to look at what they offer and make sure it tallies with what they are looking for.

When choosing a trainer, it is worth asking if you can pop along to one of the classes (without your dog) to get a feel for what they do and how they do it. Most trainers will be happy to accommodate this as it means they have a potential client. It also means that an owner is more able to decide whether or not that particular class is for them.

Another method would be to sign up to a workshop, again, often workshops will have a dog attendance element and spaces for people to attend without their dog. This is a good opportunity to see the trainer at work and decide if they are the ones to work with the dog going forward.

As previously mentioned, each trainer will have an area which they specialise in, and therefore it follows that an owner with a specific issue will not get satisfaction from attending training classes which are focused on unrelated elements. For example, if an owner with a highly reactive dog attends a class for medium to advanced obedience, they will quickly find themselves feeling as though they are making little to no progress as the set up for the class may well be unsuitable for the dog that they have. Instead, by taking time and doing the research an owner is more likely to find a trainer that will be able to effectively help them.

Most trainers are highly qualified in their areas of expertise; however, the standards of qualification can vary quite considerably. It is possible for someone to take an online course which lasts a few months and then set themselves up as a trainer, they may be an incredibly good trainer and perfectly suited to doing the job, however, they may equally be running classes a bit too soon in their understanding, and subsequently the quality of the advice is limited and their ability to deal with all dogs is restricted. It is also worth pointing out that some trainers may have qualifications coming out of every orifice, yet still be unable to help an owner with their specific problem. This is why it is vital to take the time and visit with a few.

Look for a membership to a recognised organisation such as the APDT, or PACT or IMDT. These organisations exist to establish a set of definable standards in dog training and membership requires the trainer to adhere to a strict set of criteria which an owner can take reassurance from when they are in attendance.

If the problem is a little more involved, then it may be that the owner requires the services of a behaviourist. Behaviourists are specialists in the effects of the dog's behaviour, and they will look at the issue and present a solution which involves both training as well as elements of behavioural management. Behaviourists, tend to work with dogs over a much longer period than a six- or eight-week training class, and will be involved in all aspects of the behavioural modification. Again, behaviourists will specialise in certain areas and practice at all levels. The fees that they charge will reflect this, Veterinary behaviourists are usually vets first with a specialist knowledge of behaviour and they are more able to help with any medical issues which may be connected to the behavioural issue.

I would generally recommend that if you have a puppy, then begin with finding a local puppy class, from there it is usually fairly easy to continue onto adult classes and potentially all sorts of other training class types, including formal obedience, ringcraft (as you would see in the show ring) agility, and a vast array of other training and exercise classes.

If you have a behavioural issue which has developed over time, the place to start would be with your vet to make sure that there is no medical reason for the behaviour to have developed, from there they might be able to help you decide if the solution is either a training one or if a behaviorist would be more appropriate, many behaviourists run training classes and workshops, and therefore the vet should be in a position to point you in the right direction. If not, contact a few trainers locally and chat with them, if they cannot help with the problem, then they often will point the owner in the right direction to get the help that they need.

Working with a trainer is a relationship in itself, as the trainer often comes to know their clients very well. Sometimes clients and trainers are not a perfect match, and the client is clearly not gelling with the trainer or the trainer's style of training. If a client does not feel comfortable with their trainer it is important that they feel comfortable enough to find another trainer as the way the owner feels about the trainer will reflect in the success, they have in that particular class. Trainers work extremely hard to ensure that everyone feels welcome, however as with all relationships it just does not work out. The important element is that the owner does not give up on training as they may find an environment more comfortable elsewhere and this is fine.

This is why I always recommend attending a class without the dog before signing up to hopefully avoid a situation where an owner finds themselves in the wrong class with a trainer they do not particularly like.

References

Book References

Kleiman, Devra G, et al,. 2010, Wild Mammals in Captivity, Principles and Techniques for Zoo Management, The University of Chicago Press, Ltd, Chicago 60637.

Miklosi, Adam, 2015, Dog Behaviour, evolution, and cognition, 2nd edition, Oxford University Press. Great Clarendon Street, Oxford, OX2 6DP

Lindsay, Steven R, 2001, Handbook of Applied Dog Behaviour and Training, Volume 1, Iowa State University Press, Blackwell Publishing Professional, 2121 State Avenue, Ames, Iowa, 50014

Lindsay, Steven R, 2005, Handbook of Applied Dog Behaviour and Training, Volume 3, Iowa State University Press, Blackwell Publishing Professional, 2121 State Avenue, Ames, Iowa, 50014

Appleby, David, et al, 2016, The APBC Book of Companion Animal Behaviour, Souvenir Press Ltd, 43 Great Russell Street, London, WC1B 3PD

Aloff, Brenda, 2002, Aggression in Dogs – Practical Management, Prevention and Behaviour Modification, Dogwise, Wenatchee, WA, 1.800.776.2665.

Pryor, Karen, 2002, Don't Shoot The Dog, The New Art Of Teaching and Training, Ringpress Books Ltd, A division of Interpet, Vincent Lane, Dorking, Surrey, RH4 3YX

Burch, Mary R, and Bailey, Jon S Ph.D., 1999, How Dogs Learn, Howell Book House, Wiley Publishing Inc., New York, NY,

Internet references

(Anon, 2021, Kennel Club website online, available at https://www.thekennelclub.org.uk/about-us/campaigns/dangerous-dogs-deed-not-breed/, accessed 21/6/2021)

About the Author

I have been working in the field of Animal welfare and training for the past 25 years and have worked with a wide range of species, from primates to wolves, However, my main area of interest is with dogs.

I have worked with dogs in various settings from training assistance dogs, through years spent working in rescue, ending up working with companion dogs in the home environment. Each dog is unique, and each dog teaches me more every time.